GEORGE WASHINGTON

25 GREAT PROJECTS

YOU CAN BUILD YOURSELF

Carla Mooney

Illustrated by Samuel Carbaugh

Build it Yourself Series

Nomad Press is committed to preserving ancient forests and natural resources. We elected to print *George Washington: 25 Great Projects You Can Build Yourself* on 4,007 lbs. of Williamsburg Recycled 30% offset.

Nomad Press made this paper choice because our printer, Sheridan Books, is a member of Green Press Initiative, a nonprofit program dedicated to supporting authors, publishers, and suppliers in their efforts to reduce their use of fiber obtained from endangered forests. For more information, visit www.greenpressinitiative.org

Nomad Press
A division of Nomad Communications
10 9 8 7 6 5 4 3 2 1

This book was manufactured by Sheridan Books,
Ann Arbor, MI USA.
September 2010, Job #320571
ISBN: 978-1-934670-63-7

Illustrations by Samuel Carbaugh

Questions regarding the ordering of this book should be addressed to
Independent Publishers Group
814 N. Franklin St.
Chicago, IL 60610
www.ipgbook.com

Nomad Press
2456 Christian St.
White River Junction, VT 05001
www.nomadpress.net

CONTENTS

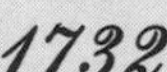

Timeline

George Washington's Life

1732
George Washington is born at Popes Creek, Virginia.

1743
George's father, Augustine, dies.

1746
Considers entering British navy, but his mother refuses to give him permission.

1748
Takes his first surveying trip to Virginia's Shenandoah Valley.

1749
Is appointed public surveyor.

1751
Sails for West Indies with brother Lawrence and contracts smallpox.

1752
Lawrence dies of tuberculosis, leaving George the Mount Vernon estate.

1753
Travels to Ohio Country to deliver message to the French stating British claims to the region.

1754
Is appointed lieutenant colonel of a Virginia regiment. Attacks Jumonville, and then surrenders at Fort Necessity.

1755
Serves as an aide-de-camp to General Braddock during a doomed campaign against the French.

1756
Commands Virginia regiment.

1758
Joins General John Forbes's expedition to Fort Duquesne. Resigns after the campaign and is elected to the Virginia House of Burgesses.

1759
Marries Martha Dandridge Custis.

1769
Observes growing British hostility toward the colonists and the imposition of more taxes by the British with increasing concern.

1773
Stepdaughter Patsy dies.

1774
Attends the First Continental Congress as a Virginia delegate.

1775
Attends the Second Continental Congress. Is chosen as the Continental Army's commander in chief and then joins the army for the siege of Boston.

1776
The British evacuate Boston and the colonists sign the Declaration of Independence. George loses battles in New York, retreats to New Jersey, and then surprises the British with a Christmas Day attack at Trenton.

George Washington's Life

1777

Wins Battle of Princeton and then moves into winter quarters at Morristown, New Jersey. The British take Philadelphia, and the Continental Army moves to winter quarters at Valley Forge, Pennsylvania.

1778

The British evacuate Philadelphia, and the British Army and the Continental Army fight to a draw at the Battle of Monmouth. The French fleet arrives.

1780

The French General Rochambeau arrives in Rhode Island, and George discovers Benedict Arnold's betrayal.

1781

The Continental Army marches south to Virginia with French troops and defeats Cornwallis at Yorktown.

1783

George calms Continental Army officers angry at the non-payment of their wages at Newburgh. Britain and the United States sign an official peace treaty. George resigns from the army and returns to Mount Vernon.

1787

Is elected president of the Constitutional Convention and signs the final version of the Constitution.

1789

States ratify the Constitution. George is elected president and takes office on April 30. George's mother, Mary Washington, dies.

1790

Congress approves Hamilton's financial plan and agrees that the capital of the United States will be on the Potomac River.

1792

Is elected president for second term.

1793

Issues a Proclamation of Neutrality when Britain and France go to war. French minister Genet stirs up trouble in the United States until the French government recalls him.

1794

Unpopular Jay Treaty signed. At home, Pennsylvania farmers take part in the Whiskey Rebellion.

1796

Issues farewell address to the nation.

1797

Retires from public office and returns to Mount Vernon.

1799

George writes his last will, freeing the slaves at Mount Vernon. After falling ill in December, George dies and is buried at Mount Vernon.

Other titles in the *Build It Yourself* series

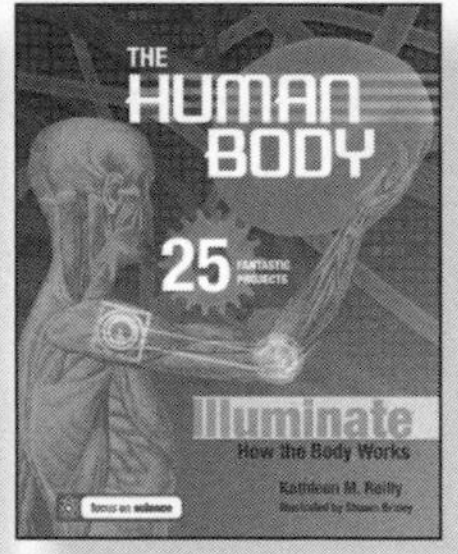

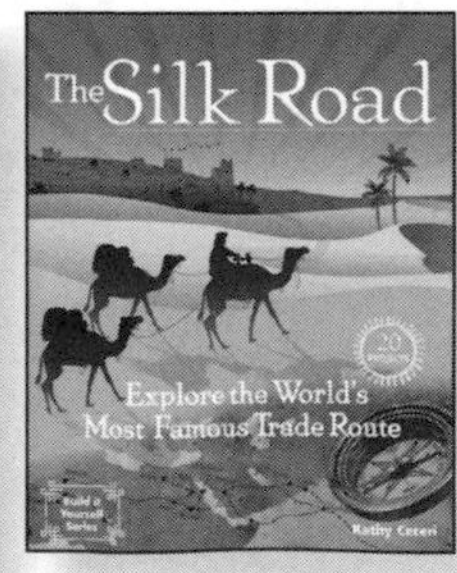

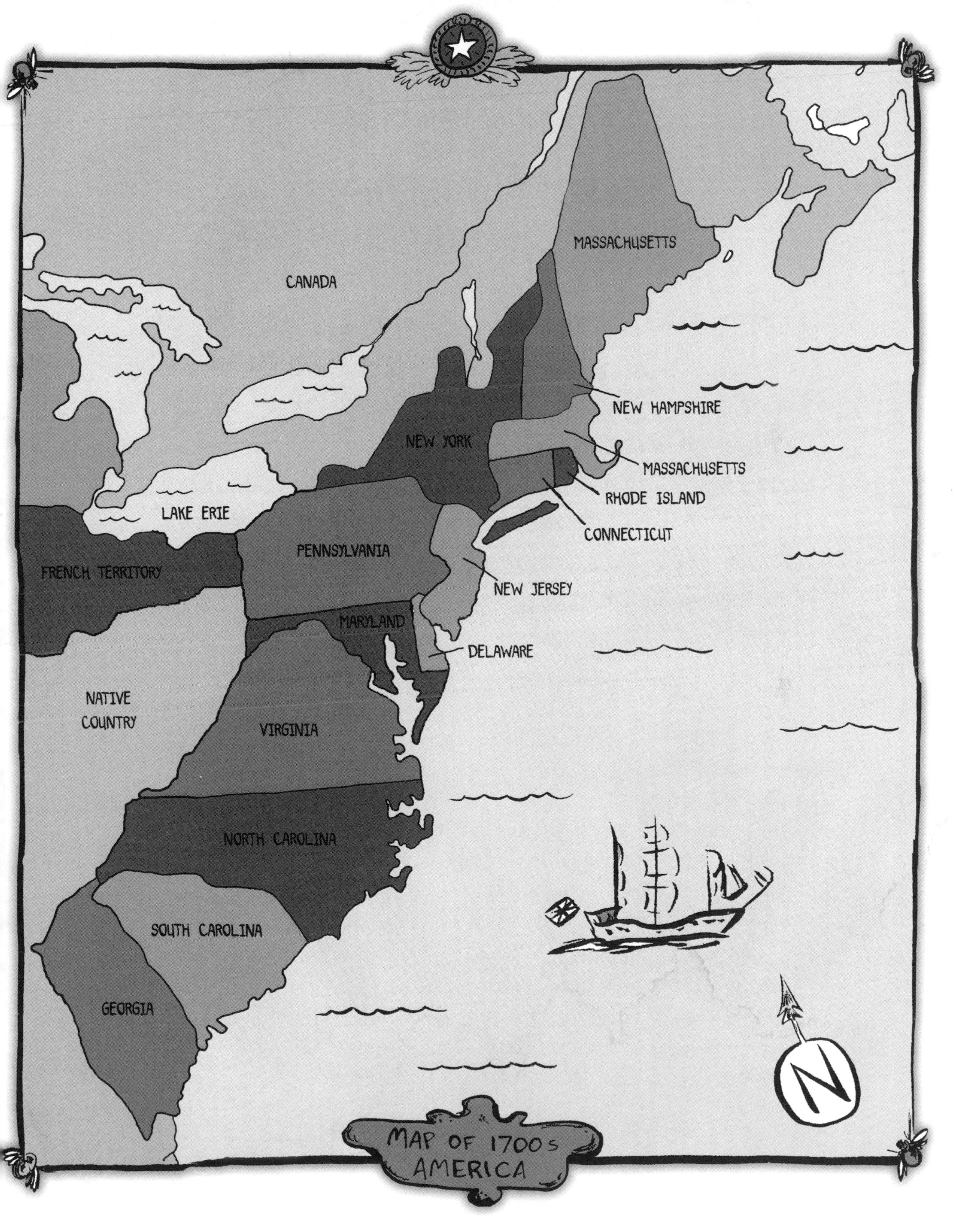

MASSACHUSETTS
CANADA
NEW HAMPSHIRE
NEW YORK
MASSACHUSETTS
RHODE ISLAND
LAKE ERIE
CONNECTICUT
PENNSYLVANIA
FRENCH TERRITORY
NEW JERSEY
MARYLAND
DELAWARE
NATIVE COUNTRY
VIRGINIA
NORTH CAROLINA
SOUTH CAROLINA
GEORGIA
N
MAP OF 1700s AMERICA

☆ INTRODUCTION ☆
George Washington

GEORGE WASHINGTON is one of the most famous Americans in United States history. In fact, without Washington there may never have been a United States of America. Without his steady hand as **commander in chief** of the **Continental Army** from 1775 to 1783, the American war for independence may have floundered from the start. Without his guidance at the **Constitutional Convention** in 1787, the states may never have united under the Constitution. Without his example as a guide, the presidency and new government might have failed miserably. George Washington was the right man, in the right place, at the right time.

But how did this legend become an American hero? Before his fame as general and president, George Washington began life as a young man in **colonial** Virginia. His humble beginnings on Ferry Farm provided valuable lessons and gave him a firm foundation that guided him throughout his life. George's courage, self-control, good judgment, and strong sense of duty would serve him well as he tackled many challenges in war and in peace.

George was an avid farmer, explorer, and devoted family man. He probably would have been content to spend his years peacefully working on his farm. However, George's sense of duty to his country called him into public service.

George's courage and honesty inspired the trust of a nation. His legend grew with each adventure. By the time of his death, George represented America and her liberty to the country and the world. He had truly become the Father of our Country.

This book will help you discover George Washington—his life, ideas, and contributions to his country. You'll learn a little history of George's time, some interesting facts about the people and places around him, and about the founding of our nation.

Most of the projects in this book can be made with little adult supervision, using materials you already have at home or can easily find at a craft store. So get ready to step back in time and discover the man who was George Washington!

WORDS *to* KNOW

commander in chief: the person in charge of a country's military.

Continental Army: the army formed by the American colonies at the beginning of the Revolutionary War. This was the war for independence from Great Britain.

Constitutional Convention: the meeting in Philadelphia at which the government of the United States was created.

colonial: the period of time when America was a group of British colonies, from 1607 to 1776.

☆ CHAPTER 1 ☆
A Young Gentleman

In February 1732, Mary Ball Washington prepared for the birth of her baby in Westmoreland County, Virginia. While her husband, Augustine Washington, had four children from his previous marriage, this child was Mary's first. In the eighteenth century, many women died during childbirth, so Mary may have been nervous as she waited for the baby's arrival. On February 22, 1732, she gave birth to a boy. Mary decided to name him after her **guardian**, George Eskridge. Thus, George Washington came into the world.

§

George was a fourth-generation Virginian. His great-grandfather, John Washington, sailed to America from England in 1657. John established the Washington family as respectable members of Virginia society. In colonial times, the amount of land a man owned determined how wealthy he was. As John built his land holdings, he sometimes took advantage of the law to claim land from Native Americans. This earned him the Native American nickname of "town-taker."

WORDS *to* KNOW

guardian: a person who protects and takes care of a child whose parents have died.

lease: rent.

orphan: a child whose parents are both dead.

old maid: a woman past the usual age of marriage.

clan: large family.

George's father, Augustine, called Gus, was born in 1694. Gus was a handsome, powerful man who stood 6 feet tall, which was quite tall in those days. People who knew him described Gus as gentle. To increase his wealth, Gus bought, sold, and **leased** lands. Eventually he achieved moderate wealth, owning 10,000 acres of land, six iron forges, and about 50 slaves.

As a young man, Gus married Jane Butler, and the couple had four children together before Jane died in 1729. After her death, Gus married Mary Ball. Mary was an **orphan** who had grown up under the guidance of a guardian. Like Gus, Mary was tall and physically strong.

When Mary married Gus on March 6, 1731, at the age of 25, she was already considered an **old maid**. After George, she and Gus had five more children: Betty, Samuel, John Augustine, Charles, and Mildred, who died as an infant. Counting George's half brothers and sisters from Gus's first marriage, the Washington **clan** numbered 10 children.

WHEN IS George Washington's Birthday?

Some people say George's birthday is February 11. Others claim it is February 22. Which is right? Actually, both are! When George was born in 1732, the colonies used an old-style calendar. At the time, George's birth fell on February 11. In 1752, the British corrected their calendar and added 11 days to the year. Under the new style, George's birthday fell on February 22.

Early Years at Ferry Farm

When George was six years old, his father moved the Washington family to a plantation northwest of Fredericksburg, Virginia. The Washington home was a one-and-a-half story house that sat on a bluff overlooking the Rappahannock River. It was called Ferry Farm because there was a ferry a short distance from the house that traveled down the river to Fredericksburg.

Ferry Farm was George's beloved boyhood home. He swam in the Rappahannock River and took the ferry to Fredericksburg. He learned how to grow tobacco, wheat, and corn in the Ferry Farm fields.

Mary Washington

Mary Ball Washington was born in 1706 in Lancaster County, Virginia. Those who knew Mary described her as rigid and formal.

George's relationship with his mother has been described as complex. He was a dutiful son who handled her financial affairs and looked out for her welfare. But he did not write or visit his mother often. When she proposed a lengthy visit to Mount Vernon, he discouraged it.

Mary was very possessive of her son. While he served in the military, she complained that he was neglecting his duty to her. Although George made sure she had money and a nice house, she embarrassed him by complaining that he had left her "in great want." Mary rarely bragged or spoke of her son's many achievements. When she died in 1789, however, Mary left George her most personal possessions and most of her estate, even though he needed it least of all his brothers and sisters.

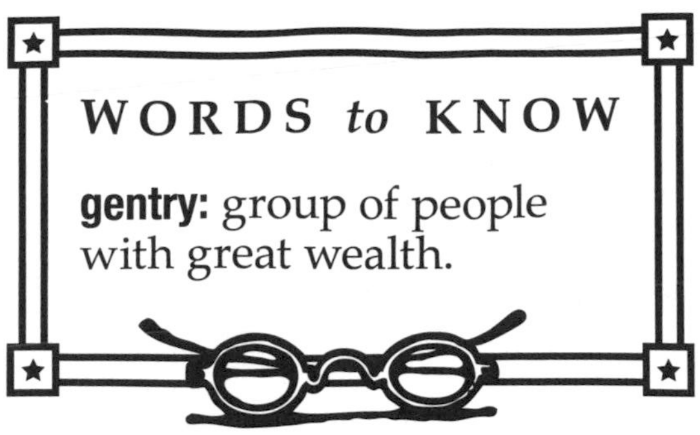

The Washingtons lived comfortably and were part of the wealthy Virginia **gentry** of landowners. As a result, George expected to travel to school in England, as his father and older half brothers had done before him.

His father's sudden death changed the course of George's life. Gus Washington died in April 1743, when George was only 11 years old. Mary Washington raised her children on her own and ran Ferry Farm with a farm manager's help. Gus's will gave most of his property to his two oldest sons, Lawrence and Augustine, Jr. Ferry Farm went to George, and Mary relied on him to help her with the farm duties and the younger children.

School Days

In colonial times, school was very different from today. Some children received lessons from tutors at home or in the tutor's home. Some schools were one-room buildings where students of all ages gathered together. The schoolmaster was usually a young man who had just graduated from college. Many children did not attend school because they were needed to help at home.

It was important for boys to learn how to read and do simple math so that they would not be cheated in business deals. Girls focused most of their education on household duties. They learned to cook, spin, knit, and sew. If they learned to read and write, they practiced their letters on cross-stitch samplers or in a recipe book.

Then & Now

Did You Know?

The childhood story about George Washington cutting down a cherry tree did not actually happen. A writer named Mason Locke Weems invented the story for a book about George.

Education

After Gus's death, Mary could no longer afford to send George to school in England, so she hired a part-time tutor for her son instead. He also attended a local school. George learned writing, spelling, grammar, math, and geography. He practiced his **penmanship**. In total, George received only an elementary school education.

George's education prepared him for his future. His geography and map-reading skills were important to his later work as a **surveyor** and army officer. George also excelled at math and **logistics**, which he used to run his **estates**. These **practical skills** later helped George lead a small, inexperienced army against the world's greatest military power.

But because he did not attend private school or college, George considered his education inferior to the formal learning of his peers. Later, some of the **Founding Fathers** looked down on George's education. Throughout his life, however, George's determination and practical skills made up for his lack of formal learning.

He always wanted to learn new things and spent hours every day reading. He read newspapers from around the country, exchanged many letters with friends, and collected a variety of books. Eventually, George's library grew to more than 700 books.

PAST PASSAGES

"That Washington was not a scholar was certain—that he was too illiterate, unread, unlearned for his station is equally past dispute."

—JOHN ADAMS

WORDS *to* KNOW

penmanship: the quality or style of handwriting.

surveyor: someone who measures land areas to set up boundaries.

logistics: the planning and organizing of details for a business or military operation.

estates: all of someone's property.

practical skills: useful skills to use every day.

Founding Fathers: members of the Constitutional Convention.

surrogate: taking the place of somebody.

Surrogate Father

After Gus's death, George's half-brother Lawrence became George's **surrogate** father. Fourteen years older than George, Lawrence was an officer in an American regiment that was part of the British Regular Army. The sight of Lawrence in his fine military uniform must have impressed young George. George dreamed of following in Lawrence's footsteps as a soldier.

Lawrence had inherited a farm on the Potomac River from their father, which he named Mount Vernon. Although George spent much of his youth at Ferry Farm, he often visited Lawrence at Mount Vernon.

Fairfax Family Influence

Lawrence's wife, Anne Fairfax, came from a nearby estate called Belvoir Plantation. Anne was a member of one of the most wealthy and powerful families in Virginia. Her father, William Fairfax, was a cousin of Lord Thomas Fairfax from England. William managed his cousin's interests in America.

Whenever George visited Mount Vernon, he spent many hours at Belvoir. Belvoir was a grand home with a library, fine furniture, musical instruments, wallpaper, and fabrics imported from England. This was George's first glimpse into a privileged way of life. It stirred his desire to acquire his own land and valuable possessions.

Did You Know?

Lawrence named Mount Vernon after Vice Admiral Edward Vernon, a British military hero who was his former naval commander.

At Belvoir, George copied the Fairfaxes' polished manners. He learned to dance and read their books. Lawrence knew George would benefit from his connection to the Fairfaxes and encouraged his brother to visit them. At the same time, however, he cautioned his brother to remember where he came from and to be careful to treat the family with respect.

The young teen quickly became a Fairfax family favorite. In particular, Lord Fairfax admired George's **horsemanship**. George could ride any horse and always rode with courage in foxhunts. The family took George under their wing. With their influence behind him, his future opportunities became significantly brighter.

Career at Sea

In 1746, Lawrence suggested that George enlist as a **midshipman** in the British navy. George was 14 years old. With the help of the Fairfaxes, Lawrence found a place for George on a British ship. Lawrence tried to convince Mary Washington that her son's future was at sea.

Mary did not like the idea of her oldest son joining the navy, but she reluctantly agreed. Then she wrote to her half-brother Joseph Ball in England and asked his advice. George's ship was about ready to sail when Mary received Joseph's reply. He advised that the navy would "cut and slash him, and use him . . . like a dog." Joseph feared that men with more influence and connections would receive promotions first. George might be stuck serving as a lowly midshipman for years. Joseph thought that George would be better off becoming a Virginia planter or a **tinker's apprentice**.

WORDS *to* KNOW

horsemanship: skill in handling and riding horses.

midshipman: an officer in training in the navy.

tinker: a mender of pots, kettles, and pans.

apprentice: someone in training.

With this advice, Mary took back her consent for George to join the navy and the British ship left without him. He would have to find his future elsewhere.

Make Your Own

Silver Plate

SUPPLIES

- sturdy paper plate
- aluminum foil
- toothpick

In George's day, talented silversmiths engraved intricate patterns into their work.

1 Cut a piece of aluminum foil larger than the paper plate. Cover the paper plate with the aluminum foil, folding the edges tightly over the back of the plate. Keep the foil as smooth as possible.

2 Carefully use a toothpick to draw a design on the foil. Do not press too hard or the toothpick will punch a hole in the foil. You can create an intricate pattern that is repeated across the plate. Or you may want to engrave the plate with a family name or crest.

WHAT IF? George Joins the Royal Navy

What if George's mother had let him join the British royal navy as a teenager? His bags were packed and his ship about to sail when she changed her mind. Her decision proved to be a lucky one for America. If George had sailed then, it is likely that Americans would not have had General Washington as their commander in the Revolutionary War. Instead, he may have been part of the British fleet blocking New York Harbor!

★ Make Your Own ★

Cup & Ball

SUPPLIES

- Styrofoam ball
- paint
- paintbrush
- construction paper
- ruler
- scissors
- tape
- string or yarn
- sturdy sewing needle long enough to push through the ball

Children in colonial America played with a wooden cup and ball toy called a bilboquet.

1. Paint your Styrofoam ball using any colors and patterns you want. Let the ball dry.
2. Cut a circle from the construction paper that measures about 9 inches in **diameter**. Fold the circle into fourths. Using the fold lines, cut out one-fourth of the circle. Form a cone with the remaining paper circle and tape the edges securely. Make sure that your cone's opening is large enough to hold your ball.
3. Cut a piece of string about 12 inches long. Thread the string through the sewing needle. Knot the end of the string.
4. Push the needle and string through the center of the ball. Pull the needle out the other side of the ball so that the string runs through the center. Pull the knot firmly against the top of the ball.
5. Push the needle through the mouth of the cone and out the tip. Remove the needle from the string and knot the string on the outside of the tip. Your ball and cup is now complete!

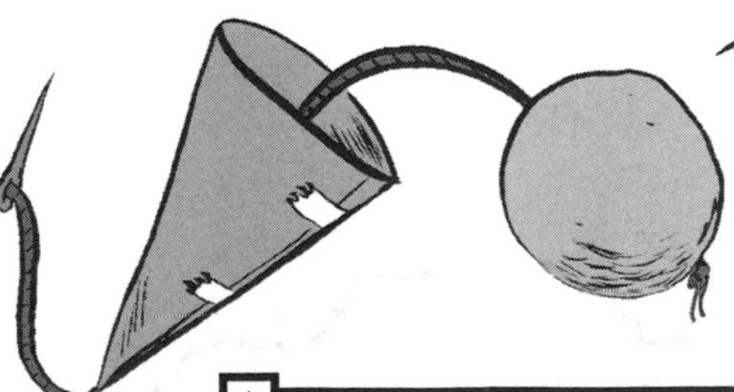

6. To play, start with the ball hanging outside of the cup. Try to swing the ball on the string into the air and catch it with the cup. To make the game harder, increase the length of your string.

WORDS *to* KNOW

diameter: the line through the center of a circle, from one side to the other.

Hornbook

Children growing up in George's time used a hornbook to learn their alphabet.

SUPPLIES

- piece of cardboard about 10 inches wide by 12 inches long
- pencil
- sturdy scissors
- paper
- black marker
- tape & glue
- plastic wrap

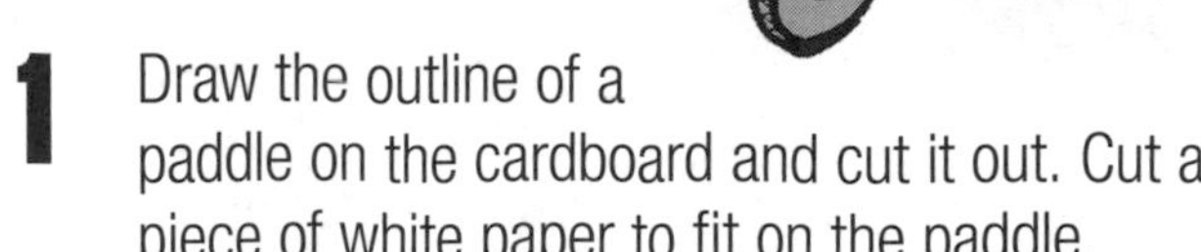

1. Draw the outline of a paddle on the cardboard and cut it out. Cut a piece of white paper to fit on the paddle.

2. Using a black marker, write the alphabet in capital letters along the top of the paper. Then write the lowercase letters along the bottom of the paper. Tape or glue the paper onto your paddle. In the middle, copy a poem or quote that you like.

3. Carefully smooth a piece of plastic wrap over the paper and secure each corner with tape.

RULES OF Civility

In colonial times, fathers taught their boys how to behave like gentlemen. With his father gone, George had to take the matter into his own hands.

As a teenager, he discovered the "Rules of Civility and Decent Behavior," a set of 110 standards for polite behavior taken from a sixteenth-century French **etiquette** manual. Some rules described how a gentleman should talk to others: "In the presence of others sing not to yourself with a humming noise." Other rules outlined how to behave in public: "Being set at meat scratch not neither spit, cough, or blow your nose except when there's a necessity for it."

George copied these instructions into his school writing book to learn social etiquette.

WORDS *to* KNOW

etiquette: accepted code of public behavior.

★ Make Your Own ★

Book of Manners

SUPPLIES

- pencil
- several sheets of lined paper
- two pieces of heavy construction paper or cardstock
- scissors
- black and colored markers
- hole punch
- three pieces of ribbon or yarn, about 8 inches each

Manners have definitely changed since the eighteenth century. Now you can decide manners for today's young ladies and gentlemen.

1 Think about what manners you believe would help young people behave politely in today's world. Jot them down on lined paper. When you have finished brainstorming, copy all of your rules neatly onto fresh paper. Use as many pieces of paper as you need. Write on only one side of the paper. Number each rule and use your best handwriting. You can decorate your pages with fancy borders if you like.

2 Cut the construction paper or cardstock to the same size as your paper. On one piece, use a pencil to sketch a fancy title for your book. This will be the front cover. Some ideas are "Rules of Behavior in Decent Company" or "Rules for Young Gentlemen and Ladies in Polite Society." When you have completed sketching the title, fill it in with black or colored marker. Add any other decorations or drawings to your cover.

3 The second piece of construction paper or cardstock is the back cover. You can also decorate this. Lay your written pages on top of the back cover and the front cover on top of everything. Make sure that it is all in the right order. Punch three holes into the side of your papers and covers, making sure that the holes line up with each other. Push a piece of ribbon or yarn through each hole and tie it in a bow. Your book is complete!

✰ CHAPTER 2 ✰

Surveyor and Landowner

NOW THAT GEORGE WAS NOT GOING TO SEA, he needed to find another way to make a living. So he decided to become a land surveyor. In eighteenth century America, land surveyors who marked property boundaries were important to the colonies. A good survey ended border disputes when two settlers argued over land. Land surveyors earned good money and were able to explore the land as they worked. For an enterprising young man like George, becoming a surveyor opened endless opportunities.

§

Surveyor's Apprentice

George's skill at math, **drafting**, and horseback riding made him the perfect candidate for land surveying. He even had his own set of surveyor's tools, inherited from his father. As George studied the art of surveying, he discovered that he had a natural talent for mapping the country before him. He practiced his surveying skills on Lawrence's property, creating several small maps.

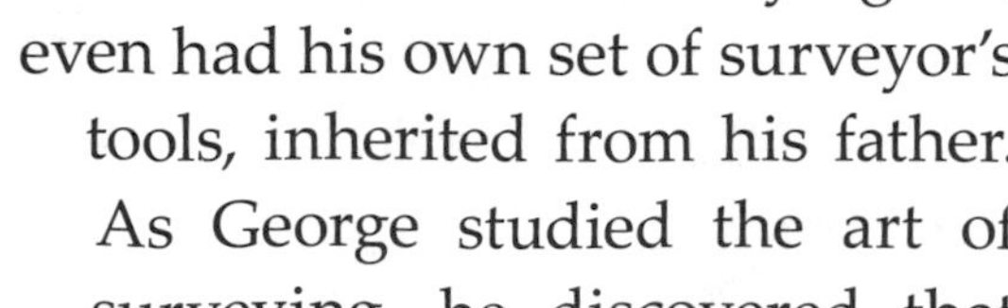

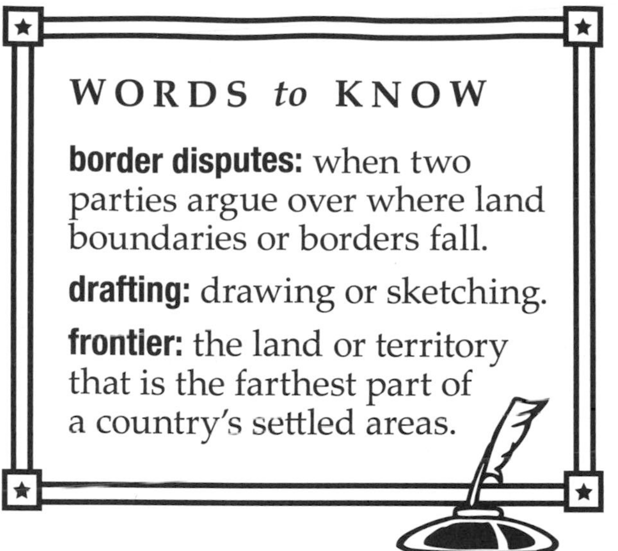

WORDS *to* KNOW

border disputes: when two parties argue over where land boundaries or borders fall.

drafting: drawing or sketching.

frontier: the land or territory that is the farthest part of a country's settled areas.

In 1747, the Fairfax family again shaped the course of George's life. Lord Fairfax held rights to more than 5 million acres across Virginia. Fairfax wanted surveys of his land. He invited George to accompany the surveyors on their trip.

In early 1748, the surveying party headed into the wilderness. The trip lasted a month as the surveyors traveled across the Blue Ridge Mountains into the American **frontier**. It was George's first real adventure—quite a contrast to the refined life at Belvoir.

During his trip, George experienced the real life of a surveyor. He swam horses across swollen rivers and ran into wild animals and snakes. He also met Native Americans for the first time, who performed a war dance for the travelers. It was the most exciting time of his life.

George had joined the trip as a 16-year-old looking for fun, but he fell in love with the western frontier. Endless acres of rich land waited to be claimed. For the rest of his life, George's thoughts would often drift to the possibilities he imagined in the West. He firmly believed that no one could stop the inevitable American move west.

Diary entry about his bed at one stop

"nothing but a little straw
matted together without sheets
or anything else, but only
one threaded Bear-blanket with
double its weight of vermin
such as lice fleas etc . . .
I made a promise not to sleep in such
a fashion from that time forward
choosing rather to sleep in
the open air before a fire . . ."

Culpeper County Surveyor

After that first trip, the Fairfaxes regularly sent George to survey their western lands. They paid him well and he enjoyed the adventures. In July 1749, 17-year-old George had enough experience and backing from the Fairfaxes to become the county surveyor for Culpeper County.

For the next three years, George surveyed and mapped almost 200 **tracts** of land. He traveled Virginia's western frontier, spending many nights sleeping under the stars. George faced poor weather, icy rivers, angry Native Americans, wild animals, and dishonest guides. Still, George was young, strong, and easily able to survive the rough, sometimes dangerous conditions of the frontier.

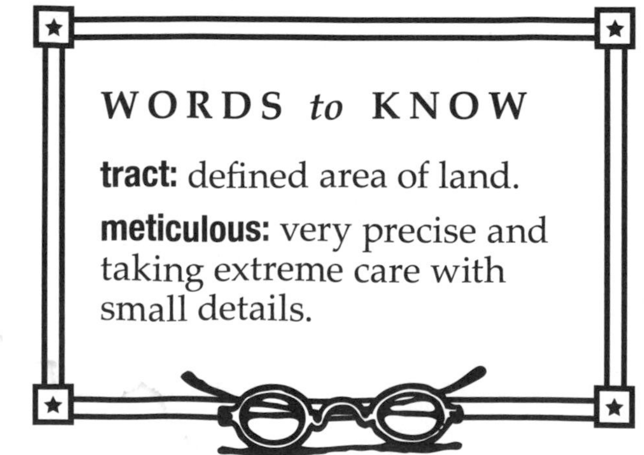

WORDS *to* KNOW

tract: defined area of land.

meticulous: very precise and taking extreme care with small details.

Landowner

With only a small inheritance from his father, George was determined to increase his land holdings. He saved his money and purchased so much land that, by his mid-twenties, he owned about 10,000 acres. With this amount of land to his name, George became an important man in Virginia society.

For the rest of his life, George would be obsessed, almost greedy, about adding new land to his holdings. His endless quest for land fueled his rise as one of the wealthiest landowners in eighteenth-century Virginia. By the time he died in 1799, his estate included more than 52,000 acres of land spread throughout Virginia, Pennsylvania, Maryland, New York, Kentucky, and the Ohio Valley. In addition, he owned property in the cities of Winchester, Bath, Alexandria, and the new capital city, Washington, D.C., which had been named after George in 1791.

Surveying required careful measurement and attention to detail and George was **meticulous**. He quickly became known for being fair, honest, and dependable. His reputation and valuable experience made him a popular surveyor. Before long, George saved enough money from his surveying work to buy his first piece of land, 1,459 acres on Bullskin Creek in the lower Shenandoah Valley.

As a surveyor, George learned valuable skills that would serve him well in his military and political careers. He discovered that organization and careful attention to detail were critical to success. He also learned how to negotiate and work with people of all backgrounds.

Did You Know?

When he was 20, George proposed to a 15-year-old girl named Betsey Fauntleroy. Her parents turned him down because they believed his future was not good enough for their daughter.

An Impressive Young Man

Although an awkward teen, George grew into an impressive young man. He stood at least six feet, two inches tall. That made him about a head taller than the average man of his time. He had an athletic build and was trim and well proportioned.

As a young man, he weighed about 175 pounds. His hands and feet were very large, giving him an awkward appearance when he stood still. Despite his large size, he was graceful while dancing and foxhunting.

George was a young man with social **ambitions**, and he dressed carefully, like an English gentleman. He refused to wear a wig because he felt it was annoying and unflattering. Instead, George tied his own reddish-brown hair back in a **cue** with a velvet ribbon called a solitaire. Sometimes, George neatly powdered his hair with a fine powder.

Sally Fairfax

Some believe that the first great love of George Washington's life was a young woman named Sally Fairfax. She came from an old, wealthy Virginia family. The oldest of four daughters, Sally was one of Virginia's most sought-after young ladies. When George was 16, Sally married William Fairfax and came to live at Belvoir. It was there that George and Sally met and developed a friendship.

During the **French and Indian War**, George wrote at least two love letters to Sally. In them, he called himself a "votary of love." He also compared himself to Juba and Sally to Marcia, characters in Joseph Addison's play, *Cato: A Tragedy.* In the play, Marcia sends away her secret lover, Juba. If they were not in love, then George was definitely flirting!

George's physical presence impressed many throughout his life. By simply walking into a room or onto a battlefield, he affected others. At the Battle of Monmouth, one of George's aides claimed that the sight of George's commanding figure stopped the men from retreating in a panic.

WORDS to KNOW

ambition: desire for achievement or distinction such as power, honor, fame, or wealth.

cue: a small ponytail at the back of the head.

French and Indian War: the war between France and England for control over the colonies in America. It lasted from 1756 to 1763.

The Man Himself

Throughout his life, George was a private and guarded man. Many thought that he had no sense of humor. That was not true! With his inner circle of friends and colleagues, George lowered his guard and showed a subtle sense of humor. He liked to hear and repeat jokes, and was known to laugh until tears ran from his eyes. One time, when George learned about the 1798 duel between James Jones and H. Brockholst Livingston, he joked, "They say the shot Jones fired at his opponent cut a piece off his nose. How could he miss it? You know Mr. Livingston's nose and what a capital target it is."

George also had a terrible temper. Few people saw its full fury because of his incredible self-control. Sometimes, however, it erupted. During the Battle of Monmouth, George is said to have cursed fiercely when he saw Major General Charles Lee retreating in the battle.

PAST PASSAGES

"He swore that day till the leaves shook on the trees.
Charming! Delightful!
Never have I enjoyed such swearing before or since.
Sir, on that memorable day
he swore like an angel from heaven!"

—BRIGADIER GENERAL CHARLES SCOTT

George's Diaries

When he was about 14, George began saving every piece of paper that belonged to him. He kept all of his letters, accounts, and other records. He started writing in a journal, with the first entry made during a surveying trip on March 11, 1748. Eventually, George arranged his growing collection of papers by date, name, and subject.

As an adult, George's obsession with his papers grew. He took his **archive** with him even when he went to war. In the army, he assigned a personal guard to protect his papers and instructed the guard to whisk the papers away to a secret, safe place if threatened. After the war, George took his papers to Mount Vernon, where his private secretary preserved and sorted the collection. The Library of Congress purchased the archive from George's heirs after he died.

Lawrence Dies

By 1751, George was nearly 20 years old and earning a good income from surveying. Still, he had larger dreams. As a child, he was awed by his older half-brother Lawrence's experiences in the British navy. George still hoped that he too could obtain a **commission** in the British military.

Lawrence was ill, suffering from **tuberculosis**, and could no longer help his younger half-brother. In September 1751, Lawrence decided to travel to Barbados, hoping that the tropical climate would strengthen him. George joined him on the trip.

This was George's first trip outside of the American colonies. While in Barbados, George caught a mild case of **smallpox**. Smallpox was a lethal killer in the eighteenth century. Fortunately, George recovered with only a few pockmark scars on his face. As a lucky survivor, he was now immune to one of the greatest killers in the American Revolution.

Barbados did not improve Lawrence's health. The brothers returned to Virginia where Lawrence died at Mount Vernon in July 1752. He left behind his wife, Anne, and an infant daughter. Lawrence's will gave the Mount Vernon estate to Anne for her lifetime, and then to his daughter. If his daughter did not live to inherit the property, Lawrence's will instructed that Mount Vernon would go to George. When Anne remarried and moved to her new husband's home, she rented the Mount Vernon estate to George.

Did You Know?

George's historical archive contains so many documents that the papers fill 124 reels of microfilm and stretch across 163 feet of shelving.

WORDS *to* KNOW

archive: an extensive record or collection of papers.

commission: a directive or assignment of an officer in the military.

tuberculosis: a deadly disease of the lungs.

smallpox: a deadly disease that leaves the skin scarred.

militia: a group of citizen soldiers; not professionals.

Lawrence's death opened a new door for George. Before his illness, Lawrence had been appointed to train the Virginia **militia** in basic skills. After Lawrence died, George asked Virginia's governor to give him the job. At the time, George had no military experience or qualifications, but he had the Fairfax support. William Fairfax assured Governor Dinwiddie that George would perform well. Eventually, Dinwiddie agreed.

At 20 years of age, George was a landowner and a successful surveyor. Now he was also Major Washington. Within the year, Governor Dinwiddie would send George on his first military mission into the western wilderness.

★ Make Your Own ★

Compass

While surveying and traveling through the frontier, George used a compass to guide him. A compass works by using the earth's magnetic field to point the compass needle toward the North or South Poles.

SUPPLIES

- sewing needle about 1 inch long
- small bar magnet
- piece of cork
- scissors
- glass or bowl of water large enough to float the cork and needle

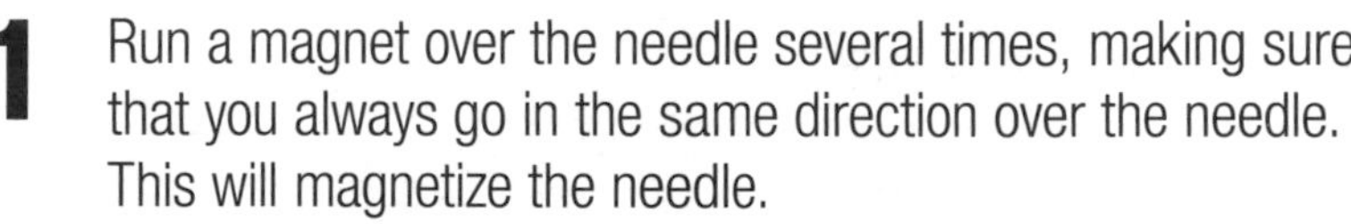

1. Run a magnet over the needle several times, making sure that you always go in the same direction over the needle. This will magnetize the needle.
2. Cut a small circle from the end of the cork. Push the needle through the cork from one side to the other.
3. Place the cork and needle in a cup of water. The needle should float almost parallel to the water's surface.
4. Place the cup on a table and watch the needle rotate. It should point to the nearest magnetic pole—north or south depending on where you live.

TRY THIS: **Put the magnet near the compass. What happens to the needle?**

Make Your Own

Quill Pen

SUPPLIES

- feather from craft store
- knife or sharp scissors
- bottle of ink or paint
- paper

In George's time, people made their pens from the feathers of ducks and other birds. These pens were called quills. To write, they would dip the end of the quill into a bottle of ink.

1. To create your quill pen, cut the end of the feather at an angle, so that you make a sharp point.
2. Dip the end of the quill pen into ink or paint. Wipe the excess ink or paint from the pen's tip on the bottle opening to prevent splatters on your paper.
3. Write a letter. See how many letters or words you can write before you have to re-dip your quill pen into the ink.

WHAT IF? George Had Not Gotten Smallpox

The American Revolution took place during a time when a deadly smallpox epidemic was sweeping through the colonies. When George first met his troops outside Boston in 1775, he discovered that 10 to 30 soldiers were dying each day from the disease. The soldiers in the American army were vulnerable because most had never been exposed to the disease in their small villages and on farms. In contrast, the British soldiers had more immunity because smallpox had ravaged Europe for generations. Most of the time, one-fourth to one-fifth of George's army in Boston was too sick to fight because of smallpox. What if George had not caught smallpox while in Barbados with Lawrence? He may have come down with the disease during the war. At best, he would have been unable to lead the troops. At worst, he could have died at the beginning of the war.

★ Make Your Own ★

Surveyor's Map

SUPPLIES

- paper
- pencils or pens
- extra-long measuring tape
- other measuring tools like rope or string
- compass

A good map includes everything that will help future map-readers identify an area. When a landowner has a survey done they are checking and marking their boundaries.

1 Take a walk outside. You can use your own backyard or go to a local park with your parents' permission. Pretend that you are seeing the land for the first time and it is uncharted territory.

2 Sketch a picture of the area. Include as many landmarks or distinguishing features as you see.

3 Decide where the boundaries of your territory will be. Mark off the boundaries and measure the area. One method is to lay your rope along boundaries and measure with the measuring tape. See what other methods you can try. Make sure to record all of your measurements.

4 After you have finished outside, add any finishing touches to your surveyor's map. Then write a detailed description of the land you surveyed to go along with the map.

5 Want to see how good your map is? Give it to a friend and see if they can find the area you surveyed based on your written description and your drawn map and measurements.

✰ CHAPTER 3 ✰
A Young Colonel

WHEN GEORGE JOINED THE ARMY, France's holdings in North America were split between Lower Canada in the north and Louisiana in the south. They wanted to link their northern and southern territories through the Mississippi River Valley. By doing so, they intended to claim this enormous region as French territory.

Virginia Looks West

The French weren't the only ones, however, who wanted this land. The number of people living in the English coastal colonies had grown at a tremendous rate. Between 1720 and 1750, the population grew from about 445,000 to 1,200,000 people. As Virginia grew more crowded, some believed that expanding the colony to the west was the perfect solution. The problem was that Virginia's far western lands bumped right into land that the French had claimed.

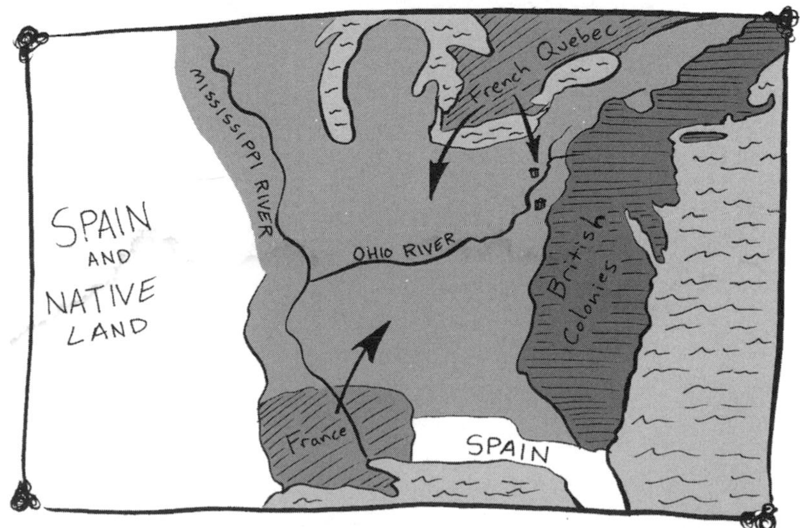

Winter Journey

When Virginia's Governor Dinwiddie heard that the French were building forts along the Allegheny River in the Ohio River Valley, he complained to England. In response, King George II commanded Dinwiddie to tell the French to leave. If they would not go, the king gave Dinwiddie permission to use force.

Dinwiddie wrote a letter that warned the French to stop intruding on English land. He had to find the right person to deliver his letter to the French commander, General St. Pierre, who was stationed at Fort Le Boeuf in northwestern Pennsylvania. The journey to the fort would cover more than 500 miles of wilderness. Dinwiddie needed someone who had enough status to serve as a royal ambassador, but also had experience in the wild.

Major George Washington fit Dinwiddie's requirements perfectly. He had influential connections through the Fairfaxes and had spent time in the Virginia wilderness on several surveying **expeditions**. Even more importantly, 21-year-old George already carried the air of someone born to lead others.

The Ohio Company

In 1747, several prominent Virginians, including Governor Dinwiddie and George's half-brother, Lawrence, established the Ohio Company. They hoped to grow rich by buying western lands in the Ohio Country and then selling them to settlers. The British government granted the Ohio Company 500,000 acres. The Company agreed to build a fort in the Ohio River Valley and encourage settlement of the area to protect British interests.

Before the Ohio Company could settle the land, the French sent several hundred men to occupy the Ohio River Valley. They nailed signs on trees and placed lead plates at points along the Ohio River. These signs and plates warned all who read them that the land belonged to France. The stage for conflict was set.

Half-King

Before reaching the French commander, George met with a Native American chief named Tanacharison. Also known as Half-King, he was a local Seneca tribe leader. Half-King complained to George about the French moving onto their lands. George knew that the British intended to claim those same lands, but did not tell Half-King. He realized that to push the French out of the Ohio Country, he would need the Native Americans on his side. He convinced Half-King to journey with him to the French fort.

In late October 1753, George's group headed out on their dangerous mission across the Blue Ridge and Allegheny Mountains into the American wilderness. They struggled through knee-deep snow and crossed rivers that were icy and swollen, forcing them to wade alongside their canoes as their clothes froze stiff. As their horses fell from exhaustion and hunger, George and his men had to leave them behind.

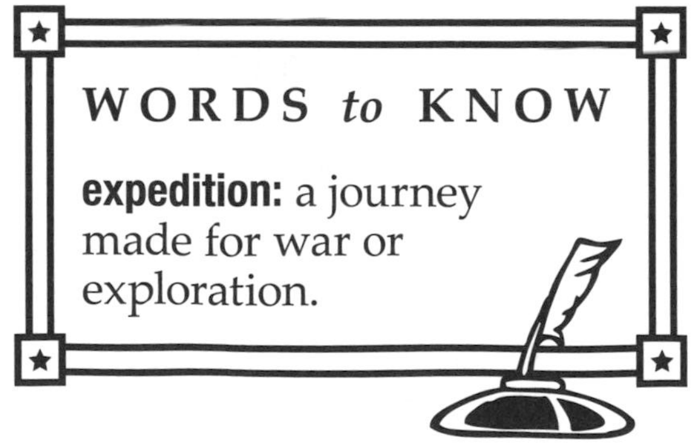

WORDS *to* KNOW

expedition: a journey made for war or exploration.

Arriving at Fort Le Boeuf, George presented Dinwiddie's letter to General St. Pierre. The General received him politely but dismissed the English claims to the Ohio Country. Despite his efforts, George's arguments had little effect on the French. He realized they would not abandon the Ohio Country unless they were forced to.

Before George left Fort Le Boeuf, he sketched a map of the fort and surrounding territory. He noticed more than 200 canoes that lay ready to carry the French down the river. George realized the French intended to make their move soon.

The return trip to Virginia was treacherous, but successful. George's ability to carry out the dangerous mission impressed many Virginians. Governor Dinwiddie published George's diary of the winter journey, and it was read throughout the colonies and even in England. The account of his adventure earned George widespread public praise.

Fort Necessity

Governor Dinwiddie convinced the Virginia **House of Burgesses** to authorize a **regiment** of 300 men to deal with the French threat. George was promoted to lieutenant colonel and became second-in-command of the force. By May 1754, George's troops reached Great Meadows, a small valley about 40 miles southwest of the French Fort Duquesne. Daily rumors of a French attack swirled in camp.

WORDS *to* KNOW

House of Burgesses: assembly of representatives in colonial Virginia.

regiment: a group of military ground forces consisting of battle groups, headquarters, and support units.

stockade: a solid fence made with strong posts standing upright in the ground.

knoll: a small rounded hill.

reinforcements: more troops.

One day, George received a message from Half-King. His scouts had spotted a small unit of French troops moving quietly in the woods. George and Half-King decided to attack the French, before the French could attack them.

They found the French party in a forest glen and a short fight broke out. George's men killed 10 French men and captured the rest. One of the men killed was the French commander, Joseph Coulon de Villiers, Sieur de Jumonville. The incident became known as Jumonville Glen.

Did You Know?

Jumonville Glen caused an international uproar. The French argued that they were ambushed while on a peaceful diplomatic mission. The Virginians claimed the French had been stalking them for days and were openly armed and hostile. They felt that their actions were justified.

After Jumonville Glen, George returned to Great Meadows and built a small fort. It was a crudely constructed, circular **stockade** named Fort Necessity, after their uncertain position. But George made a mistake. He expected the French to charge across the open fields, and did not pay much attention to the tree-covered **knolls** that looked down on the fort.

As George and his men waited for **reinforcements** to arrive, he tried to convince the local Native Americans to fight with him. But they predicted a British defeat and deserted George. Before he left, Half-King warned George that his fort would be useless in any battle. But George was inexperienced and did not listen to the leader's wise advice.

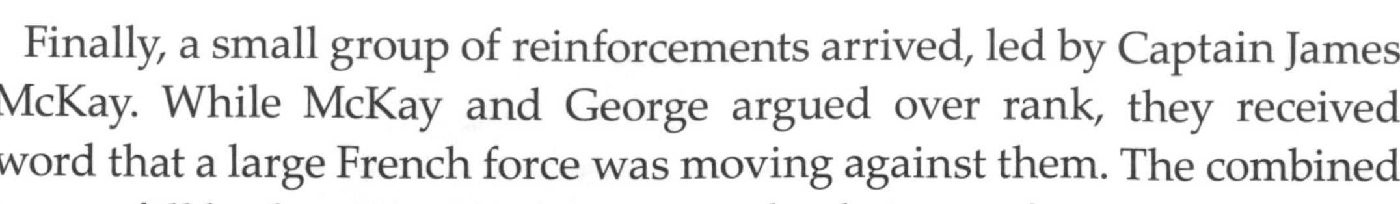

Finally, a small group of reinforcements arrived, led by Captain James McKay. While McKay and George argued over rank, they received word that a large French force was moving against them. The combined troops fell back to Fort Necessity to make their stand.

On July 3, a French force of about 1,100 soldiers and Native Americans appeared around Fort Necessity. They settled on the tree-filled knolls and took advantage of the protected higher ground. Hiding behind trees and stumps, the French rained musket fire down upon the fort.

The slaughter continued for nine hours. George ran around the fort and gave orders to his men as he stepped over the dead and wounded. In the afternoon, a driving rain fell from the skies. It filled the trenches with bloody water and leaked into the gunpowder stores, making the powder useless.

As dusk began to settle over the fields, the French offered a ceasefire. One-third of George's men had been killed or wounded. There was little food or useable gunpowder left to continue a stand. George realized that his position was hopeless. He surrendered.

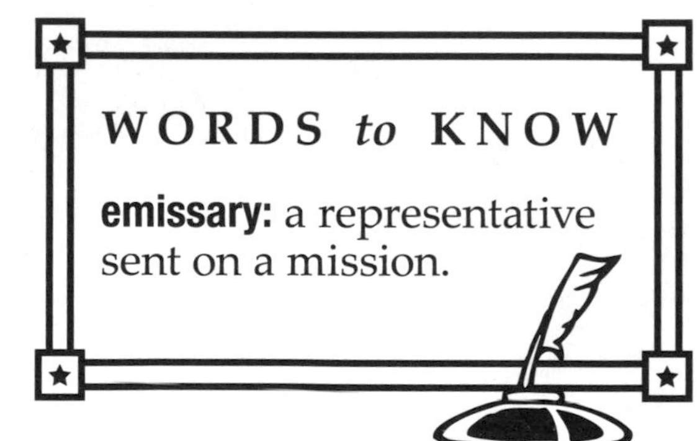

WORDS *to* KNOW

emissary: a representative sent on a mission.

Surrender at Fort Necessity

The commander of the French force was Louis Coulon de Villiers, brother of the dead Jumonville. He presented a document, the "Articles of Capitulation," that George signed as part of his surrender. Written in French, the surrender document included an admission that George and his troops had assassinated Jumonville, a diplomatic **emissary** of the French government. Later, George claimed he received a poor translation of the document. He said that he never would have signed the document if he had known it contained the assassination admission. Regardless, the damage was done.

After the surrender, the French allowed George and his men to march out of Fort Necessity. Slowly, they headed home to Virginia.

The defeat at Fort Necessity had enormous consequences. The French called George a villain who murdered a peaceful diplomat and then tried to cover it up. George became famous as the man who started France and England's Seven Year War that lasted from 1756 to 1763. Many Native Americans took the lopsided defeat at Fort Necessity as a reason to side with the French. The British officers viewed the entire event as an example of incompetent colonial forces.

In Virginia and the colonies, however, the reaction was much different. The stand at Fort Necessity was seen as a noble attempt to block the French from invading Virginia's western land. The House of Burgesses gave Colonel Washington and several of his men a public thanks for their brave efforts in the face of great odds. George emerged from the event with greater public standing.

PAST PASSAGES

"The volley fired by a young Virginian in the backwoods of America set the world on fire."
—HENRY WALPOLE

George had hoped that his service would help him earn a commission in the regular British army. But the commission never came. The Virginia House of Burgesses decided not to fund a new mission against the French. Not only would the regiment be broken up into smaller companies, no colonist would have a rank higher than captain. If George stayed, he would be demoted from colonel to captain!

WORDS *to* KNOW

demotion: reduced to a lower grade or rank.

aide-de-camp: a military officer who acts as an assistant to a superior officer, usually a general or admiral.

siege: surrounding and attacking a fortified place, like a fort, and cutting it off from help and supplies.

ambush: a surprise attack.

allies: people who join together to help each other.

George was devastated. Rather than accept a **demotion**, George resigned from the army in November 1754. He returned to Mount Vernon, determined to turn his efforts to farming and his lands.

General Braddock

After George's defeat at Fort Necessity, France sent several thousand soldiers to America to reinforce their troops. The British responded by sending General Edward Braddock and two British regiments to the colonies. General Braddock was a decorated war veteran with more than 40 years of military experience. All of his battles, however, had been fought in the traditional European style, in which armies faced each other on an open field, in line formations. This time, he would have to lead a mission in the wilderness.

Braddock's orders were to force the French from the land Britain claimed. Shortly after his arrival in February 1755, Braddock planned a march to take Fort Duquesne. When George learned of Braddock's arrival and mission, he realized he had an opportunity to learn from Braddock's vast experience. George wrote to Braddock, requesting to serve on his mission. George volunteered as an **aide-de-camp** and joined Braddock's men in May 1755.

IN HIS WORDS
To his brother

"they were halting to Level every Mole Hill, and to erect Bridges over every brook; by which means we were 4 Days getting 12 Miles."

Braddock prepared a massive force to lay **siege** on Fort Duquesne. About 2,500 horses pulled wagons loaded with heavy cannon, supplies, and food for 2,000 troops. The entire group stretched for over six miles. Progress with such a large, cumbersome group was slow. The troops cut their own road through the wilderness as they went.

Early on, George sensed disaster. The slow pace meant they were in danger of being **ambushed** by the French or Native Americans. Already, stragglers were being killed and scalped on a regular basis. This told him that the local people and probably the French knew about their movements. If they did not move more quickly, the French would have time to reinforce Fort Duquesne. George advised Braddock that a faster group of men should be sent ahead of the main force. Braddock agreed and ordered an advance group to move forward.

Braddock's Arrogance

In many areas, Braddock refused George's advice. As the army marched, Native American **allies** appeared. When they offered to help in the upcoming battle, George urged Braddock to accept. Braddock, however, offended the Native Americans and they quickly left. In addition, Braddock's advance group had stretched into a thin line for several miles. George worried about being ambushed. He recommended sending scouting parties ahead of the troops. If an ambush waited ahead, the scouts could discover it and warn the main body. Braddock disagreed. He believed that a group of Native Americans or French hiding in the woods might scare colonial forces, but not his British regulars.

On July 8, an advance force of Braddock's troops arrived within 12 miles of Fort Duquesne. As the British soldiers marched forward, they felt confident of victory.

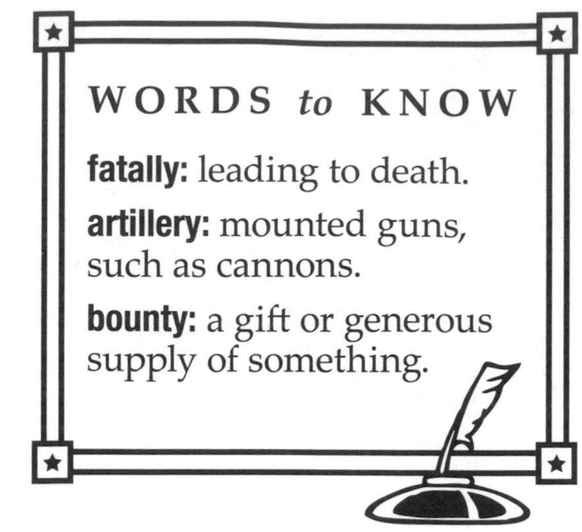

Meanwhile, the French had received regular reports about Braddock's march. They knew they were outnumbered and their best chance was to ambush Braddock's force. After persuading the Native Americans to join them, they gathered a force of about 900 men. They picked a spot about 7 miles from the fort and waited in ambush.

As the British troops moved from the heavy forest into a small clearing, musket balls rained down upon them. Only blue smoke rising from muskets revealed that the firing came from the trees. The Brits tried to fire back at the unseen targets, but it did little good. The Native Americans were excellent marksmen and the red uniforms of the British made easy targets. The British huddled in little groups, firing blindly. Before long, dead and wounded soldiers filled the ground.

The Virginia soldiers found trees to stand behind while firing. This Native style of fighting angered Braddock. He ordered that none of his troops use trees to protect themselves. As he rode to rally his troops, Braddock was **fatally** wounded.

As the battle raged, George rode through the fighting. His majestic figure on horseback was a tempting target for the enemy. Two horses were shot out from underneath him. A musket ball shot off his hat. Four bullets tore through his coat, but George remained unharmed. As men fell around him, no bullet, tomahawk, or arrow touched George. Later, Native Americans would testify that they had tried to shoot George, but it was as if an unseen force protected him.

PAST PASSAGES

"I may point out to the public that heroic youth, Colonel Washington, whom I cannot but hope Providence has hitherto preserved in so signal a manner for some important service to his country."

—REVEREND SAMUEL DAVIES

The massacre lasted over two hours. With Braddock and the other officers wounded or killed, it was up to George to rally the survivors and retreat. He organized the remaining Virginians to provide cover to the retreating British regulars. The British abandoned everything to the enemy, including wagons, guns, **artillery**, horses, and money.

George led the surviving men 40 miles in the dark night. During the retreat, near Great Meadows, Braddock died from his wounds. George instructed the men to bury him in the road. Then they ran wagons over the fresh grave to disguise Braddock's burial spot from the enemy. The French and Indians, however, did not pursue the British retreat. They were too busy enjoying the **bounty** left by the British on the battlefield.

By July 17, George and the army reached Fort Cumberland in Maryland. Braddock's mission was a complete disaster, with 900 men killed or wounded. Word of the shocking defeat quickly spread throughout the colonies.

IN HIS WORDS

To his mother, describing the English soldiers

"...struck with such a panic, that they behaved with more cowardice than it is possible to conceive."

George wrote to his mother and brother, assuring them of his safety. In his letters, he expressed his dismay at the defeat.

Upon his return to Virginia, George was a hero. Fellow officers and soldiers praised him for his courage and quick decisions during the raging battle. Braddock drew the blame for the defeat, while George emerged with praise and honor.

Braddock's defeat taught George several important lessons that he would remember years later. He realized that the size of Braddock's troops and supplies worked against them. More importantly, he saw that the British method of fighting did not work in the American wilderness. The forest-fighting methods of the local people were far superior.

WHAT IF? Braddock Lived

Had General Braddock lived, George's future may have taken a completely different path. Before the campaign, Braddock promised that he would secure a position for George in the British army. There is no reason to believe that he would not have kept his word. George would have finally received his long-desired position in the British army. The Revolutionary War may have had a drastically different outcome with General Washington fighting for the British!

Virginia Commander

After Braddock's defeat, the British abandoned the Ohio Country to the French and their Native American allies. This left the western borders of Virginia and her frontier settlements vulnerable to attack. To defend this land, the Virginia Assembly authorized an army of approximately 1,200 to 2,000 men. They voted 23-year-old George as colonel of the Virginia Regiment and commander of all Virginia forces. It would prove to be a hands-on learning experience that would prepare him for the challenges he later faced during the Revolutionary War.

Did You Know?

Another survivor of Braddock's defeat was Captain Thomas Gage. Twenty years later, at the beginning of the Revolutionary War, George would again meet Gage as the commander of the British army.

To his brother John

"We have been most scandalously beaten by a trifling body of men."

Over the next three and a half years, George recruited, trained, and led the Virginia Regiment. He trained his men in the polish and discipline of the British army as well as in the agility and practical know-how of Native American fighters. They patrolled the Virginia frontier, engaging in **skirmishes** with Native American **raiders**. George learned that keeping his army fed and armed required constant effort and attention to detail.

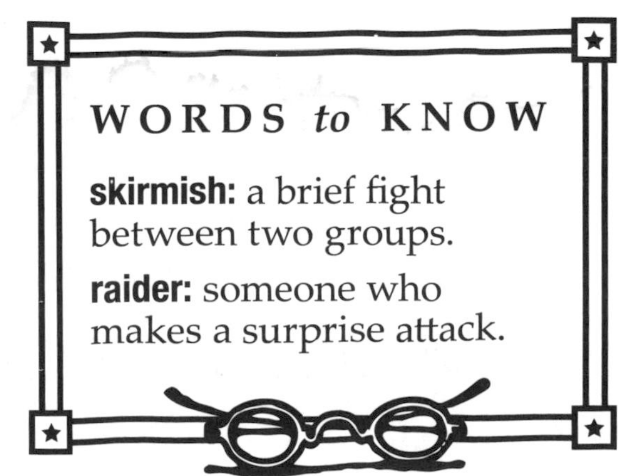

George's mission was next to impossible. Native Americans had greater numbers and the element of surprise on their side. George tried to persuade some of them to ally with the English, but most remained in support of the French.

Forbes Campaign

By 1758, the British decided to try to regain control of the Ohio Country. In April, George learned that General John Forbes was leading a mission to capture Fort Duquesne. Forbes had more than 30 years of experience in the British army. His force would be more than twice the size of Braddock's. George requested an introduction to Forbes, hoping to join the campaign. Forbes welcomed Colonel Washington and the Virginia Regiment to join his force of approximately 8,000 British regulars and colonial troops.

By November, George and Forbes' force reached the outskirts of Fort Duquesne. This time, there was no battle. Discovering that they were greatly outnumbered, the French had abandoned the fort and left it burning. It was a victory for the British, although not the glorious battle they had anticipated.

The French decision to abandon the Ohio Country effectively ended the French and Indian War for George. Virginia's western lands were now safe. Giving up his dream of obtaining a British commission, George returned to Mount Vernon.

Good Advice

Forbes heeded George's advice in several key areas. He agreed to use Cherokee allies as scouts. He adopted the ranger uniforms of the Virginia regiment so that the red coats would not be easy targets. He also agreed to train his forces in forest fighting tactics, something that Braddock had refused to allow.

★ Make Your Own ★

George Washington Sword

SUPPLIES

- piece of cardboard about 20 inches long
- pencil
- X-acto knife
- green and gold paint
- paintbrush
- aluminum foil
- tape or glue

During the Forbes Campaign, two Virginia regiments mistook each other for the enemy and started firing. George rode between them and knocked up rifles with his sword in order to stop the firing. Despite riding in the middle of two firing lines, not a single bullet touched George.

1. Sketch the shape of a sword on your cardboard, using a pencil. Use the X-acto knife to cut it out along the edges.
2. Paint the handle—called the hilt—of the sword green. Paint the bottom and top of the hilt of the sword gold.
3. Add thin, horizontal silver stripes to the green handle. Keep the stripes evenly spaced.
4. Once the paint has dried, wrap aluminum foil around the blade of the sword to give it a metallic look. Use tape or glue if needed.
5. Now grip your sword and flash it through the air. Are you ready to join George Washington's regiment?

Make Your Own

Spyglass

Colonial soldiers and spies used these small, hand-held telescopes to watch enemy movements.

SUPPLIES

- 2 paper tubes from paper towel or toilet paper rolls
- scissors
- tape
- paint
- paintbrush
- construction paper
- glue
- pen
- ruler
- X-acto knife
- wooden sticks, drink stirrers, or popsicle sticks

1 Before you begin, make sure that one paper tube just fits inside the other. If they are the same size, cut along the length of one tube and tape it with a little overlap to make tube's diameter smaller. Decorate your paper tubes using paint or construction paper.

2 Cut a strip of construction paper about ½ to 1 inch wide and glue it around the end of your outer tube.

3 Place the inner tube inside the outer tube. Use tape to secure the tubes so they don't move during the next step.

4 Use the pen to make four marks on the outer tube. Marks 1 and 3 should be across from each other. Marks 2 and 4 should be across from each other. Using the ruler, draw straight lines from each mark down the length of the large tube. Each line should stop about ½ inch from the tube's top and bottom edge.

5 Have an adult stand the tube up on one end and cut four slits along the lines with an X-acto knife. Make sure the knife goes through both tubes.

6 At the end of the large tube opposite the band of construction paper, insert a wooden stick into slit 1 and out of slit 3. Trim it (if necessary) so that it sticks out about a quarter inch on each side. Insert a second stick into slit 2 and out of slit 4. It should also stick out a quarter inch on each side.

7 Extend your spyglass by pulling the inner tube out as far as it will go. It will feel stiff the first few times you move it. If your wooden sticks move too much, place a piece of tape on the outside of the tube to shorten the slit.

Make Your Own

George Washington Hat

SUPPLIES

- pencil
- blue, yellow, and white construction paper
- scissors
- glue
- stapler

George Washington wore a three-cornered hat called a tricorn hat. It was made of wool. Wealthy men decorated their tricorn hats with lace, feathers, and silver and gold. The three turned-up sides caught the rain and directed it back over the shoulders of the person wearing it.

1. Draw the outline of one side of your hat on blue construction paper. Cut it out and use it as a guide to trace and cut two additional sides. You will have three sides in all.

2. Trace and cut out decorations for your hat. Use the white construction paper to make a border along each top edge of your hat's three sides. Other decorations include circles, stars, and stripes. Glue the white border along the top edge of the three hat sides. Glue other decorations as well.

3. When all sides are decorated, staple the edges of two sides together. Next, staple the third side to one of the open ends. Complete a triangle by stapling the last two remaining ends together.

✰ CHAPTER 4 ✰

At Home in Virginia

AFTER RETIRING FROM THE MILITARY, George returned home to Mount Vernon. He was determined to live a private life as a Virginia farmer. His thoughts turned to his western lands and plans to expand his farms. As a young man, they also turned to marriage.

George and Martha

In the spring of 1758, George began **courting** a young widow named Martha Dandridge Custis. Martha was a tiny woman, standing close to five feet tall. She had large hazel eyes, dark brown hair, a strong curved nose, and tiny feet and hands. Her friendly charm made her well liked by most who met her.

Martha's first husband, Daniel Parke Custis, left her a rich estate that included several plantations, slaves, and silver money. She was one of Virginia's wealthiest **widows**.

George and Martha married on January 6, 1759. The marriage may have been a **strategic union**. He took control of her lands and she found an able manager. Even so, George and Martha also shared a quiet love and respect for each other. George treated Martha as a lady and followed her opinion and wishes on many matters. For her part, Martha tended to George's comfort and career. Much of their relationship remains a mystery. After George's death, Martha destroyed most of their letters, keeping their relationship permanently private.

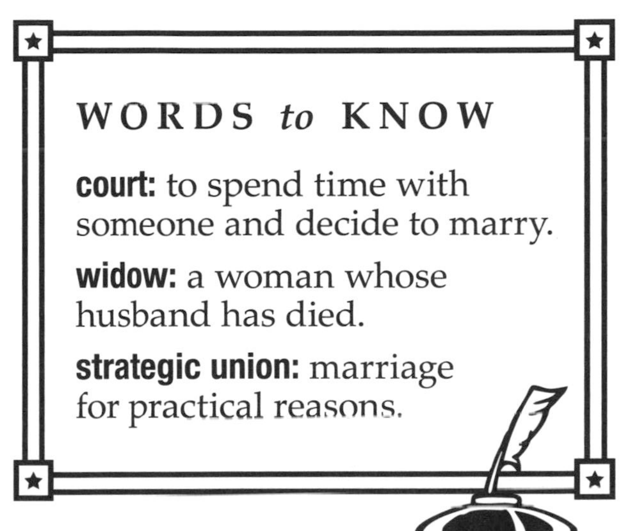

WORDS *to* KNOW

court: to spend time with someone and decide to marry.

widow: a woman whose husband has died.

strategic union: marriage for practical reasons.

George Washington's Teeth

Like many people in the eighteenth century, George began losing his teeth in his twenties. By the time he became president, he had only one tooth left. George's problems with his teeth caused him a lot of pain and discomfort. Some historians believe that his puffy jaws in portraits were the result of dental problems. Eating, drinking, and talking must have been difficult and painful for him. He frequently endured toothaches and infections that led to teeth being pulled. At one point, George bought teeth from slaves and tried to have them transplanted into his mouth. George also used at least six different sets of false teeth over the years. He tried false teeth made of hippopotamus ivory, gold, lead, animal teeth, and human teeth.

Stepfather to Jacky and Patsy

Martha had two children from her first marriage: four-year-old Jacky and two-year-old Patsy. George was a devoted and responsible stepfather. He made sure that the children had the best toys, clothes, and opportunities. His annual orders from London always included something for the children. For Jacky, he ordered silver shoe buckles and a silver-laced hat. Each year, Patsy had a new baby doll. Jacky also had a personal servant, a private tutor, and a horse and hounds for foxhunting.

Did You Know?

A great sadness in George's life was that he never fathered his own child. George would have no heir for the Washington name and property.

IN HIS WORDS

About Patsy

"This sudden and unexpected blow . . . has almost reduced my poor wife to the lowest ebb of misery,"

Sadness struck when Patsy fell ill at age 12. Doctors diagnosed her with epilepsy. They tried many methods to cure her and manage her disease. Despite their efforts, Patsy suffered a seizure and died one night in 1773. Patsy's death devastated Martha and George.

After Patsy's death, Martha became more protective of her son. George allowed her to dote on Jacky and did not interfere. Jacky grew into a spoiled and lazy young man. He resisted George's efforts to give him the best education, one that George never had.

WORDS *to* KNOW

octagonal: eight sided.

cupola: a dome-like structure on a roof, sometimes housing a bell or lantern.

portico: a structure with a roof and columns, like a porch.

Mount Vernon

Lawrence's widow died in 1761. Because her daughter had already died, George inherited the Mount Vernon estate. The estate was a series of farms totaling about 2,126 acres, each with its own slaves and overseer.

When George had first come to live at the estate, the Mount Vernon house was a simple, four-room farmhouse.

As George prepared to marry Martha, he began a series of renovations that would transform the house. First, he added a second story and wings on either side of the original house. Later additions included a distinctive **octagonal cupola** on the roof. He also added a large **portico** that ran the entire length of the house and had a spectacular view of the Potomac River. George's renovations transformed the Mount Vernon farmhouse into an impressive 18-room mansion.

Did You Know?

When George died he left Mount Vernon to his nephew. After several generations, the Mount Vernon Ladies' Association of the Union purchased the estate. Since that time, the society has restored and cared for the estate. In 1960, Mount Vernon was designated a National Historic Landmark.

George also designed the outlying buildings, such as the servant quarters, laundry room, washhouse, smokehouse, kitchen, and slave quarters. Around the mansion, George planted lawns and gardens. He built a bowling green on the front lawn for games after dinner. George's vision created a park-like setting for Mount Vernon.

Over the years, George also bought adjoining land to enlarge the estate. By the time the Revolutionary War began, the estate held about 6,500 acres. Mount Vernon became one of the best run and most desirable estates in the colonies.

Did You Know?

Most Virginia planters sold their tobacco to a British agent who would resell it in Britain. George realized the entire system favored the British agents. Because the agents controlled the price of tobacco and the price for British goods, it is not surprising these arrangements often ended with the planter owing money to the agent.

America's First Farmer

George enjoyed his role as a Virginia farmer. This love of farming remained with George all of his life. As he gathered honors during the Revolutionary War and served as the nation's first president, George still thought of himself as a Virginia farmer.

Farming was in George's blood. His father and brother before him farmed Mount Vernon. Like many Virginians, they planted tobacco, which was a crop that had made many Virginia landowners rich. At first, George also planted tobacco. But tobacco plants used the nutrients in the soil without replacing them and slowly destroyed the land upon which they grew. After years of tobacco planting, the fields wore out.

WORDS *to* KNOW

gristmill: a mill for grinding grain.

cooperage: a place where barrels or casks are made.

distillery: a place where grains such as wheat and corn are processed into alcohol.

diversify: to produce many different crops or goods.

schooner: a type of sailing ship with two or more masts.

IN HIS WORDS

To a friend about farming

"my agricultural pursuits and rural amusements . . . have been the most pleasing occupation of my life, and the most congenial to my temper, notwithstanding that a small proportion of it has been spent in this way."

George decided to grow wheat and corn instead. He built a **gristmill** at Mount Vernon to grind his crop into flour that could be sold in Alexandria or Norfolk. George's fine flour became known as the best in the colonies. George's mill included a **cooperage** that made barrels and a **distillery** to make valuable whiskey out of his grains.

By studying the best English farms, George learned it was important to **diversify** his crops. In addition to wheat and corn, he planted grains like rye, barley, and oats. He set up fruit and vegetable gardens at his farms. He also created fields for cattle and hogs. To take advantage of the Potomac River, George built a **schooner** to fish for herring and shad. He then purchased a ship to carry his flour and fish to distant markets.

By 1775, Mount Vernon was a thriving, self-sufficient estate. The farms produced enough food to feed the Washingtons and all of their slaves. It also generated income from wheat and other items.

Improvements on the Farm

Throughout his life, George constantly worked to make his farms better. He experimented with the latest farming methods and improved the tools and buildings used at his farms. In his usual custom, George kept diaries full of farming practices, weather patterns, and experiments. Other American farmers learned by watching George's success at Mount Vernon.

Colonial Bathrooms

Unlike today, colonists did not have the luxury of indoor bathrooms. Instead, they used outdoor bathrooms called outhouses, privies, or necessaries. These were small buildings located away from the house. The outhouse did not have modern plumbing or toilets. Instead, there was a simple board placed over a hole in the ground. In addition, there was no toilet paper. Colonists used other materials such as leaves, moss, or newspaper.

Then & Now

PAST PASSAGES

"He has about 4,000 acres well cultivated and superintends the whole himself. Indeed his greatest pride now is, to be thought the first farmer in America."

—JOHN HUNTER

If George had not been called away from Mount Vernon by the Revolutionary War and his presidency, he may have become known as one of the colonies' most **visionary** farmers. This **legacy** probably would have pleased him. A visitor to the Washington farm, John Hunter, noted George's passion for his farms in 1785.

Slave Owner

Eighteenth-century Virginia relied on slave labor. At first, George did not oppose slavery. He inherited slaves from his father and added more as he increased his lands and when he married. At one point, George owned as many as 300 slaves.

As George's farms moved away from tobacco production, which required a lot of labor, he did not need as many slaves. That posed a problem for him, because many of his slaves married and had children. George was unwilling to break up families by selling slaves to different owners. This meant that George kept many slaves that he did not need. At the time of his death, only about 100 of his 300 slaves regularly worked on the Mount Vernon estate.

Over time, slavery made George more uncomfortable. He began to think that it was not right for one human to own another. He saw the slave trade system as cruel and unnatural. In the war, thousands of black soldiers served under him. They impressed him with their courage, loyalty, and refusal to desert the Americans for the British, even after the British promised them freedom.

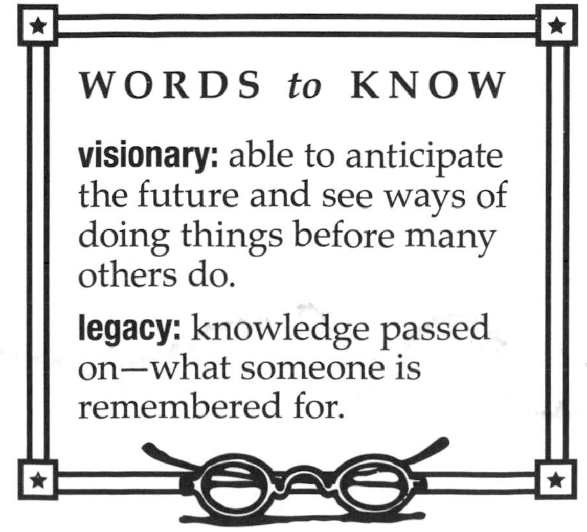

WORDS *to* KNOW

visionary: able to anticipate the future and see ways of doing things before many others do.

legacy: knowledge passed on—what someone is remembered for.

Billy Lee

George developed a close relationship with one slave. He bought William "Billy" Lee in 1767 and made him his personal servant. For years, Billy Lee served at George's side, often joining George on hunts. He traveled with George during the Revolutionary War. After Billy broke his knees, he was unable to continue serving as George's servant. In the late 1780s, he retired to Mount Vernon as a shoe cobbler and stayed there for the rest of his life. George considered freeing Billy, but he would have had no place to go in Virginia. George's death and will, however, would eventually grant Billy his freedom.

As slavery declined in the north, George noticed that the northern economy did not fall apart. Instead, it grew strong and prosperous. It was proof that an economy did not need slavery to succeed.

George hoped that slavery could be abolished peacefully. In his time, several northern states had abolished slavery. Slavery was not yet deeply established in the South. What George did not realize, however, was that the rise of cotton plantations would make the Deep South very dependent on slave labor. There would be no peaceful freedom.

Hobbies

Although George was fascinated with farming, he also spent many pleasant hours enjoying hobbies and amusements. George enjoyed foxhunting with neighbors or visitors. After the hunt, the men usually joined George at Mount Vernon for dinner and perhaps a game of cards. Whether at cards or horse races, George sometimes gambled small amounts of money. In his usual practice, he kept detailed records about each bet and his winnings and losses.

George was also an excellent horseman. He rode, bought, bred, and traded horses his entire life.

Although George could not sing or play an instrument, he loved music. He and Martha often attended balls. George also hired a music teacher to give lessons to Patsy and Jacky at Mount Vernon when they were young. He bought the children several instruments, including a spinet, violin, flute, harpsichord, and English guitar. George and Martha also regularly attended plays in Alexandria, New York, and Philadelphia.

Religion

George was a member of the Anglican Church in Virginia. Like many men of his class, he performed his duty as a vestryman, or member of the church's council. He did not, however, attend church services on a regular basis. He kept his personal religious beliefs to himself and rarely wrote about them in his many letters and papers.

Although George's personal views were private, he believed that religion played an important role in the community. He respected many different religious views, unlike many men of his time.

George as a Freemason

In the 1750s, George joined the Masonic Lodge of Fredericksburg. Freemasonry was a secret fraternity dedicated to brotherhood and the belief in a Supreme Being. Although Freemasonry was not a religion itself, it encouraged members to follow their own religious beliefs. Several Founding Fathers, including Benjamin Franklin and John Hancock, were also freemasons. As with church services, George did not attend Masonic meetings regularly.

Pursuit of Western Lands

In addition to supervising his farms, George continued to add land to his holdings. During the French and Indian War, proclamations from Virginia and England gave land grants to **veterans**. George believed that he was entitled to land under both grants and pursued his claims.

In 1763, King George issued another proclamation that closed the western lands to American settlers and made the land into a reservation for Native Americans. George felt that no king across the ocean could stop the Americans from moving west. On this issue, George claimed his independence from England.

Beginnings of a Political Career

In 1758, George had joined Virginia's House of Burgesses. His entry into politics was quiet. Much of his attention was still at home, focused on his wheat crops, Patsy's health, and pursuing land claims. This would change as the tensions between the colonies and Britain grew.

In the mid 1760s, Britain and the colonies argued over taxes and control. The French and Indian War had been expensive and the British Parliament thought the American colonies should pay for part of it. They claimed they had the right to tax the American colonies.

The idea of taxation caused an uproar in the colonies. When Britain issued a series of taxes including the **Stamp Act** of 1765 and the **Townshend Acts** of 1767, colonial protests were loud and clear.

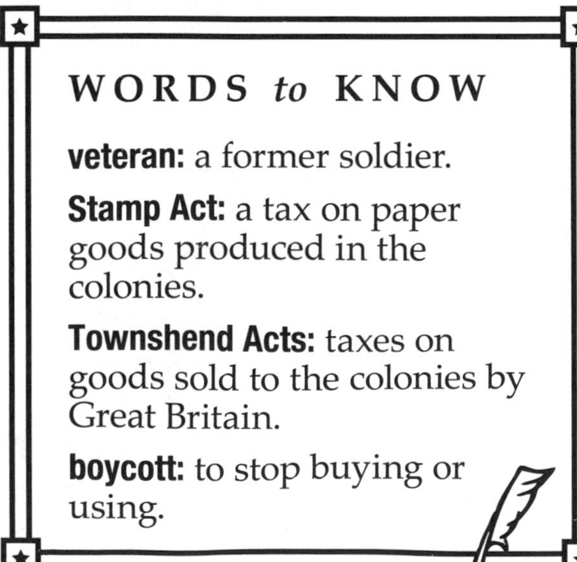

WORDS *to* KNOW

veteran: a former soldier.

Stamp Act: a tax on paper goods produced in the colonies.

Townshend Acts: taxes on goods sold to the colonies by Great Britain.

boycott: to stop buying or using.

The colonies had a common interest for the first time, uniting them against Britain.

At first, George stayed quiet during the public debate on taxation. He hoped a peaceful solution could be found. By 1769, however, George could no longer hold his tongue. He presented a plan to the Burgesses to **boycott** British goods. It hit the British in the wallets and encouraged Virginians to reduce their economic dependence on Britain. George worried about the increasing hostilities between the colonies and Britain. They appeared stuck in an endless cycle of taxation and protest. Still, George clung to the hope that the two sides could find a compromise.

George's hopes were dashed in 1773 when he read about events in Boston. In response to the tax on tea, a group of colonists boarded three tea ships and threw the tea into Boston Harbor. This event became known as the Boston Tea Party. It caused the British to issue a series of laws called the Intolerable Acts in 1774. One of the acts closed Boston's harbor while another allowed British soldiers to occupy Boston. To George and many others, the events in Massachusetts set the colonies marching toward revolution.

IN HIS WORDS

About taxation uproar

If the cycle continued,
"more blood will be spilt on this occasion,
if the [British] ministry are determined to
push matters to the extremity,
than history has yet furnished
in the annals of North America,"

★ Make Your Own ★

Pomander

SUPPLIES

- orange (or apple or lemon)
- toothpick
- whole cloves
- plastic ziptop bag
- cinnamon
- plate or paper towel
- ribbon, about 18 inches long

Pomanders are ornaments made from oranges and cloves. They made colonial homes smell nice. People hung them around the house or gathered them in a bowl.

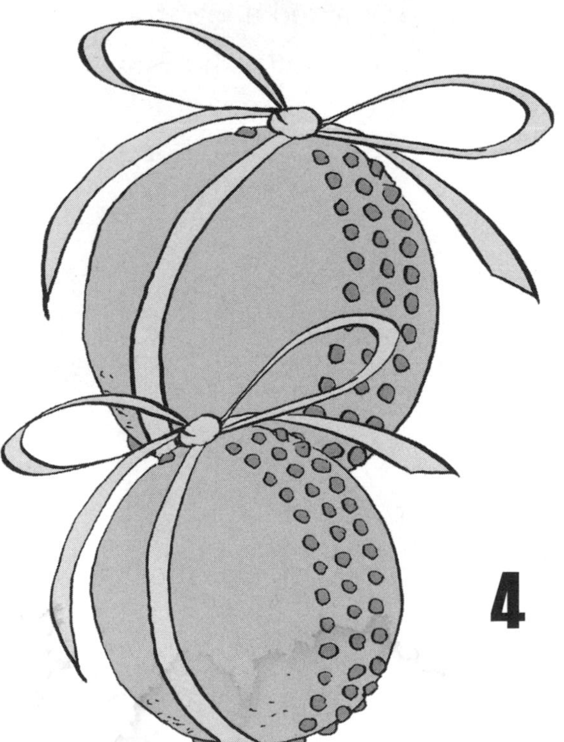

1 Using the toothpick, poke holes in the orange. Push the pointy end of a clove into each hole, letting the top of the clove rest on the orange skin. You can place the cloves randomly or create a pattern.

2 When you have finished inserting the cloves, place the orange in a plastic ziptop bag. Add a small amount of cinnamon and shake the bag to coat the orange.

3 Carefully remove the cinnamon-covered orange from the bag and place it on a plate or paper towel. Tap to remove the excess cinnamon.

4 Wrap the ribbon around the orange and tie a bow at the top or make a loop for hanging the orange. Now set the orange in a cool, dry place for several days. It is ready to use throughout the house when it is hardened.

Weather Vane

Weather vanes help people predict the weather by pointing in the direction of the wind. They often topped barns and farmhouses and were made of wood, iron, and copper. In 1787, George Washington added his own weather vane in the form of a dove at Mount Vernon.

SUPPLIES

- 2 pieces of heavy cardboard about 18 by 18 inches
- pen or pencil
- X-acto knife or heavy scissors
- black and red or copper paint
- paintbrush
- piece of sponge
- tape
- ¼-inch dowel rod
- newspaper
- plastic soda or water bottle or plastic quart-size milk bottle
- sand

1. Sketch the design for your weather vane on one piece of cardboard. You could choose a dove for your weather vane, or pick a design of your own. Some common weather vane subjects are whales, birds, and boats.

2. Cut out your weather vane. Ask an adult for help with the X-acto knife. Trace and cut out a copy of your weather vane from the second piece of cardboard.

3. To make your weather vane look like it's made of iron, paint it black. Then sponge red or copper paint around the edges to mimic rust spots. Paint the opposite side of the other piece of cardboard in the same way.

4. When the paint has dried, securely tape the two unpainted sides of the weather vane together. Leave space in the middle for the dowel to go in.

5. Make a newspaper funnel to pour sand into your bottle. Fill the bottle about three-quarters full. Push your dowel into the sand. When the wind blows, your weather vane should spin and point into the wind.

★ Make Your Own ★

Colonial Apron

Women and children wore aprons in the eighteenth century to protect their clothing while they worked. Some decorative aprons were made of fine material and embroidered.

SUPPLIES

- kitchen towel or rectangular piece of cloth
- sewing needle
- thread
- fabric glue (optional)
- ruler
- safety pin
- ribbon, long enough to tie around your waist in a bow
- lace (optional)
- decorations

1 If the edges of your towel or fabric are not hemmed, sew or glue a small hem on the bottom and sides so that the apron does not fray.

2 At the top of the apron, fold over about a quarter inch of fabric, and then fold over about three-quarters of an inch of fabric. Make sure you fold to the back side of the apron. Sew or glue the folded edge to the body of the apron. This will make a small casing at the top of the apron.

3 Attach the safety pin to the end of the ribbon. Using the safety pin as a guide, thread the ribbon through the apron casing until it comes out the other side.

4 If you to make a decorative apron, glue or sew lace around the edge to make it fancy. You can also glue or sew on other decorations. Tie the ribbon and apron around your waist with a bow!

Make Your Own

Hoecakes

SUPPLIES

- large bowl
- mixing spoon
- 2 cups self-rising cornmeal
- 2 eggs
- 1 tablespoon butter
- ¾ cup milk
- ⅓ cup water
- ¼ cup vegetable oil
- skillet
- stove
- butter or shortening
- spatula
- honey & butter

George Washington's typical breakfast included hoecakes with butter and honey, and tea. Hoecakes are a type of pancake made with cornmeal. During colonial times, they were often baked in a fireplace on the blade of a hoe, giving them the name hoecakes!

Did You Know?

George Washington is one of the most painted and sculpted men in American history. His first portrait was painted by Charles Wilson Peale in 1772. George felt extremely uncomfortable and silly sitting for the painter.

1. Measure and mix all the ingredients in a large bowl. Heat the skillet on the stove and grease it with butter or shortening.
2. Spoon the batter onto the hot skillet and lightly press it with your spatula. Flip the hoecake when the bottom turns golden brown. Cook both sides until brown and crispy.
3. Eat the hoecakes with butter and honey, just like George!

☆ CHAPTER 5 ☆

Commander in Chief

ALARMED AT THE CRISIS UNFOLDING IN MASSACHUSETTS, the colonies called a meeting in Philadelphia. Each colony sent a delegation to this meeting, known as the First Continental Congress. Together, the colonies hoped to find a solution to the disputes with England.

Continental Congress

George traveled with the Virginia delegation to Philadelphia in September 1774. For most meetings, George remained silent and listened to the other men debate. The delegates agreed that only the colonies had the right to **legislate** and impose taxes. They thought the British taxes went against the colonists' rights. To protest, Congress voted for more boycotts against Britain.

George agreed that the colonies should legislate themselves. While British taxes outraged many people, George thought taxation was only one part of the problem. The king's attempt to close the western frontier to colonial expansion struck George closer to his heart. In George's mind, this symbolized the conflict between the colonies and the British government. Whose rights were more important? The people living here or the rulers across the sea? Until this question was settled, there would be no peace.

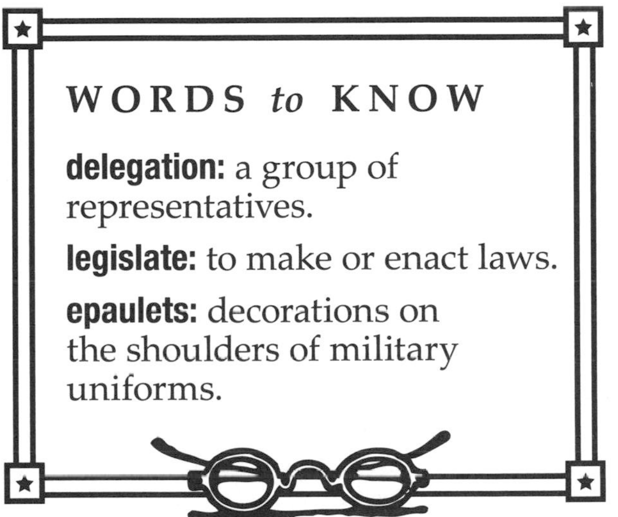

WORDS *to* KNOW

delegation: a group of representatives.

legislate: to make or enact laws.

epaulets: decorations on the shoulders of military uniforms.

Although George hoped for peace, he prepared for the worst. Before leaving Philadelphia for home, he bought a new sash and **epaulets** for his military uniform and ordered a book about military strategy.

Hostilities Rise

Back at Mount Vernon, George settled into familiar routines, but kept an eye on the news about the looming crisis. A Second Continental Congress was announced in May 1775, and George set out once again for Philadelphia. He did not know it at the time, but he would not return to his home for many years. When he reached Philadelphia, news arrived of fighting between the British and the colonists in Lexington and Concord, Massachusetts. "The shot heard 'round the world" had been fired.

George arrived at the Second Continental Congress in his full military uniform. He listened as the delegates eventually agreed to raise an army of soldiers from Pennsylvania, Maryland, and Virginia to join the New Englanders. Now they needed a commander.

The Congressional delegates must have noticed George's majestic figure. Now in his early forties, George drew men to him with his charm and leadership. His quiet manner gave an impression of strength and wisdom. George was a war veteran who was young enough to lead a new campaign. Even better, George was a Virginian. A Virginia commander with a New England army united North and South. The vote was unanimous. On June 16, 1775, the Continental Congress officially invited George Washington to command the Continental Army.

Did You Know?

George wrote Martha about the events in Philadelphia and his misgivings about the task ahead. The idea of 13 separate colonies uniting to defeat the world's greatest military power seemed impossible. George knew that if he and the army failed, he could be hanged as a traitor and his beloved Mount Vernon taken by the British.

George doubted his ability to take on this monumental task. He had never commanded a force larger than a regiment. Compared to the British officers he would face, George was completely unprepared. Yet there was no one in the colonies better suited for the job. George agreed to accept only reimbursement of his expenses.

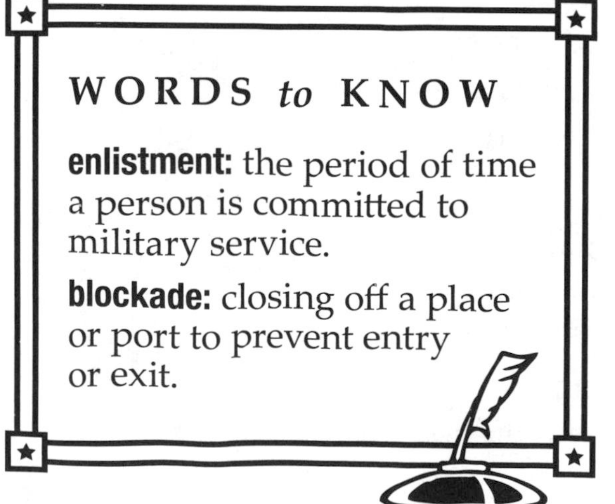

Taking Charge of the Army

George reached the army outside Boston on July 3, 1775. The 14,000 troops consisted mostly of men on short-term **enlistments** from local militia. Many would leave as their terms expired at the end of 1775. For the entire war, numbers would be an issue for George. His battle force was usually far below 10,000 men.

George also found the army short on supplies. They needed guns, ammunition, uniforms, blankets, and tents, but there was little money available to purchase these items. In fact, it took George almost a year to get one blanket for each of his men! There was often no pay for the men. While George was happy to volunteer, the men were not. From time to time, pay shortages caused the men to riot and protest. Dealing with the constant shortages took up much of George's time.

George was convinced that the cause was right. The colonies had always governed themselves. Now Congress was their lawful government. One of the Americans' greatest strengths was their belief in their cause. George worried, however, that this passion would not be enough to win a long, drawn-out war.

George's Asset

Self-conscious about his lack of formal education and military experience, George surrounded himself with a strong group of men. Men like Alexander Hamilton, Henry Knox, and the Marquis de Lafayette became close advisors. George treated his staff well and trusted them. Most were fiercely loyal to him. In this one area, George had the advantage. In everything else, including guns, soldiers, and money, the British held the upper hand.

Siege of Boston

When George joined his army in Massachusetts, he found that the British had taken control of Boston. In response, the Americans surrounded the city with a **blockade** and the two armies settled into a standoff.

For eight months, the siege dragged on. Both the British and the Americans needed time to organize and get supplies. Finally, the Americans planned a strike after a northern army led by Benedict Arnold and Ethan Allen captured the British fort of Ticonderoga and gained control of a large number of cannons.

George ordered that the American army work through the night to place the cannons on Dorchester Heights, hills that overlooked Boston. The British awoke to find themselves surrounded by cannons pointing straight at them. After a few days, the British abandoned Boston and sailed away.

The Americans cheered George's first Revolutionary War victory. It was a needed boost to morale. George had wanted to engage the enemy in battle, but the Continental Army was in no shape to meet the strongest fighting force on Earth. If a direct battle had been fought, George and the Americans may have lost the entire war during its first few days.

Defeat in New York

The British sailed for New York City. They could use their superior fleet of ships in the rivers and harbor around the city. By taking New York, the British could cut off New England from the rest of the colonies.

George marched his army toward New York. He did not have enough men to defend the city, but abandoning New York would deal a tremendous blow to the fragile American morale. George and Congress agreed that the city had to be defended as best as possible.

While Thomas Jefferson was drafting the Declaration of Independence in Philadelphia, George prepared for the coming engagement with British General Howe's forces. But George made a critical mistake.

He divided his troops between Long Island and Manhattan, placing each in a vulnerable position. Smallpox weakened the Americans further, striking one-fourth of the soldiers.

The British ships arrived in New York harbor in early July 1776 and about 33,000 troops landed on Staten Island. As George watched the British build-up, he received a copy of the Declaration of Independence on July 6, 1776. When the Declaration was read aloud in camp, the army cheered. The war's cause had officially changed. The Americans were no longer fighting for their rights as British subjects. Now they fought for their independence.

Despite their enthusiasm, inexperienced Americans proved to be unprepared for battle. Many of them turned and ran when facing British guns. After a series of defeats in New York, White Plains, and Fort Washington, what was left of George's army slipped across the Hudson River and fled through New Jersey and into Pennsylvania.

The defeats in New York were devastating for the Americans. Passion for independence was not enough to sustain troops who were no match for the British in hand-to-hand battle. The Continental Army was seriously wounded. Unless George could quickly raise a new army, he warned, "I think the game is pretty near up."

Did You Know?

A strike from General Howe at this point could have ended the war. In the eighteenth century, however, many European armies did not fight during winter. Instead, they hunkered down to wait for spring. The British missed a great opportunity.

Surprise at Trenton

After his New York defeats, George knew that the army and the colonies needed a victory to raise morale. Discovering that a **garrison** of **Hessian** soldiers was camped at Trenton, New Jersey, George came up with the brilliant plan to strike their camp on Christmas Day. He personally led his tired, hungry men in boats across the ice-filled Delaware River. The crossing took longer than expected and only one unit made it across, but it was enough. The Americans completely surprised and surrounded the Hessians. George followed up with another surprise strike a few days later at Princeton.

For the first time since the war began, George used his army's strengths. They could move twice as fast as the British and could think for themselves. Quick strikes like Princeton were ideal.

The victories at Trenton and Princeton did not seriously harm the British troops. But they lifted American spirits. After New York, the cause had appeared lost. Now there was hope. In addition, the victories caught the eye of Britain's old enemy, France. They sent badly needed supplies to the Continental Army.

George began to understand that the Americans did not have to win this war. They simply needed not to lose it. If the fighting lasted long enough, British support for the war would fade and help might come from France and Spain. Time was on his side.

Did You Know?

When George's army encountered the British at Princeton, he rode on his horse between the two lines. As both sides fired, George's aides feared for their commander's life. But when the smoke cleared, George sat unharmed on his horse while men lay wounded and dying around him.

Winter Months

That winter, George made two important decisions. To combat the smallpox that was ravaging his ranks, George made smallpox **inoculations** mandatory. Second, he decided to fight a defensive war. This strategy did not come easily to George. He thought withdrawing showed weakness. He realized, however, that the Continental Army was no match for the British. If the Americans were to win, they had to survive.

Fall of Philadelphia

In 1777, General Howe and his British troops moved toward the American capital of Philadelphia. While George wanted to meet Howe's army, his generals reminded him that his army's safety was more important. George reluctantly agreed. Howe occupied Philadelphia on September 26, then joined the majority of his troops near Germantown.

Studying the enemy's positions, George planned a surprise strike similar to the one at Trenton. On October 4, 1777, George's force approached Germantown at night and arrived near dawn. At first, the battle went well for the Americans. Then heavy fog and battle smoke confused them. In the chaos, some fired on their own men, and the British troops gained control. The Americans retreated, but Howe did not pursue them, losing another opportunity to destroy George's army.

George kept the army alive to fight another day. As 1777 ended, Howe settled into comfortable Philadelphia accommodations. George and his men prepared to spend the winter about 25 miles away, in Valley Forge, Pennsylvania.

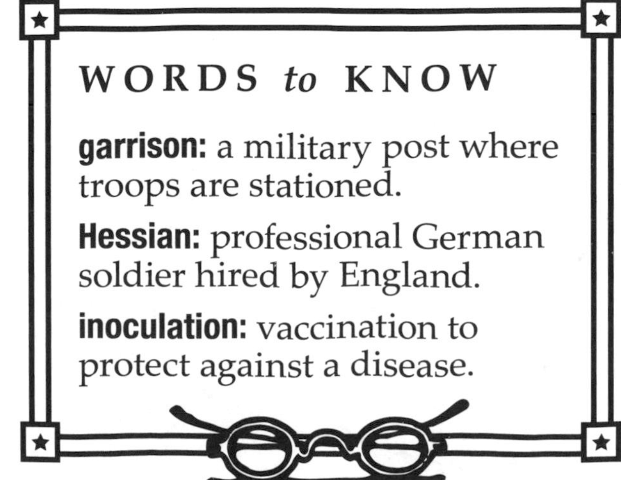

WORDS *to* KNOW

garrison: a military post where troops are stationed.

Hessian: professional German soldier hired by England.

inoculation: vaccination to protect against a disease.

Victories in the North

Around the same time George's army faced the British outside Philadelphia, the northern division, led by General Horatio Gates, scored a victory in upstate New York. After a series of battles, British General John Burgoyne surrendered nearly 6,000 men to Gates on October 17, 1777, at Saratoga.

Some men compared George's failures to Gates's success in New York. Gates was a former British officer who thought himself superior to George. He wanted George's job and openly snubbed his commanding officer by sending his reports directly to Congress. Gates also refused direct orders from George to send reinforcements to Pennsylvania.

The comparison to Gates bothered George. He already felt he had failed by letting Philadelphia fall to the British. He longed for a decisive battle to redeem himself. For weeks, he tried to find a way to strike Philadelphia and retake it. But without reinforcements from Gates, George's force was too small and an attack would have been foolish. Here, George showed amazing self-control and common sense. He placed the survival of the army above his pride.

Misery at Valley Forge

That winter in Valley Forge was filled with hardship and illness. Often, the soldiers had nothing to eat but a bit of fried dough. To protect themselves from the cold, the men built shelters with log walls, dirt floors, and smoky fireplaces. In addition, diseases such as typhoid, pneumonia, dysentery, and typhus ran through the camps. As a result of the conditions, approximately 2,000 men died in camp.

Did You Know?

During the winter months, Martha traveled from Mount Vernon to join George. Her presence raised his spirits. She and the other women in camp took care of the sick and wounded men, cooked meals, and made everyone as comfortable as possible.

The Upside of Valley Forge

At Valley Forge, one good thing emerged. The Baron Freidrich Wilhelm von Steuben, a Prussian general, volunteered to help the Continentals. He trained the soldiers and drilled them endlessly. All the while, he made the lessons fun. The men enjoyed his over-the-top giddiness when maneuvers went well and his dramatic rages when they did not. During those long winter months, the Americans learned the military skills they lacked.

Somehow, the Continental Army managed to emerge from Valley Forge intact. In the spring, George received a piece of good news. France had recognized American independence and planned to offer support. It was a small light of hope in a dark time.

Battle of Monmouth

British General Howe had spent the winter of 1778 in the comfort of Philadelphia. As spring arrived, he seemed in no hurry to attack George's army at Valley Forge. Angered by Howe's indulgent lifestyle, his superiors in London sent over a replacement.

Sir Henry Clinton was a hesitant man. When he heard of a French fleet sailing to America, he feared he would be surrounded. He abandoned Philadelphia in June and moved his army back to New York.

When George received word of the British movement, he decided to strike from the rear. Second-in-command Charles Lee was given leadership of the engagement.

IN HIS WORDS

About Valley Forge

"To see Men without Clothes to cover their nakedness, without Blankets to lay on, without Shoes, by which their Marches might be traced by the Blood from their feet, is a mark of Patience and obedience which in my opinion can scarce be paralleled."

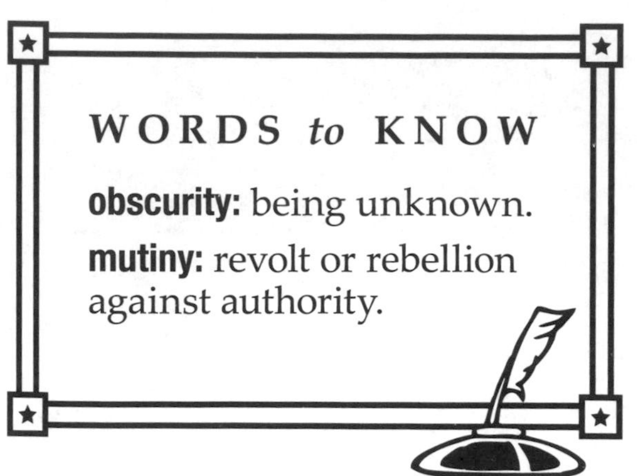

WORDS *to* KNOW

obscurity: being unknown.

mutiny: revolt or rebellion against authority.

Lee's men ran into the British army near Monmouth Court House in New Jersey. George heard the sounds of battle, but then silence. Was the battle over already?

As George rode forward to investigate, he ran into Lee's retreating men. The astonished General Washington confronted Lee and the two men argued angrily. When Lee offered excuses for his retreat, George relieved Lee of his command on the spot.

George quickly stopped the retreating soldiers and re-formed the men into ranks. The Americans fought bravely that day and the British finally retreated toward Manhattan.

Monmouth was the last great battle of the Revolutionary War to be held in the North. It cemented George's reputation as a great military commander. Meanwhile, Charles Lee was found guilty of disobedience and neglect of duty. He retired from the army and faded into **obscurity**.

Marquis de Lafayette

At Valley Forge, George came to know a young Frenchman, the Marquis de Lafayette. The 19-year-old nobleman volunteered with the army, as had several French officers. Most of the French walked around camp with a superior air, which irritated George. Lafayette, however, impressed George with his courage in battle and his eagerness to learn. George came to trust Lafayette and included him in his inner circle of advisors. Later in the war, George gave Lafayette command of the Continental troops in Virginia. Over time, the two men formed a deep bond, like father and son.

"General Washington seemed to arrest fortune with one glance. His presence stopped the retreat. His graceful bearing on horseback, his calm and deportment which still retained a trace of displeasure were all calculated to inspire the highest degree of enthusiasm. I thought then as now that I had never beheld so superb a man."

—MARQUIS DE LAFAYETTE

PAST PASSAGES

Battles in the South

After Monmouth, the British turned their eyes south. About 8,000 soldiers sailed from New York to Charleston, South Carolina. They captured Charleston in May, taking almost 5,000 prisoners. It was the Continental Army's worst defeat to date. The British rampaged through South Carolina, defeating Horatio Gate's army at Camden.

George wondered if there would be a home left for him after the war. The country was tired and its resources drained. The army was weak and on the verge of **mutiny**. Only a decisive victory would turn the tide.

Fortunately, a French army of about 5,000 troops had arrived under the command of Count de Rochambeau and set up camp in Rhode Island. A few months later, in the spring of 1781, George received word that a French fleet was headed for the American coast. George hoped to convince the French to join him in attacking New York. But he also drew up plans for an alternate attack in the South.

Benedict Arnold's Betrayal

In August 1780, George placed his good friend Benedict Arnold in command of the garrison at West Point in New York State. West Point was key to the American defenses. It blocked the British advance on the Hudson River and to the north.

But Arnold had become bitter and disillusioned with the American cause. He was also influenced by his pretty young wife who favored the British. He agreed to hand West Point to the British in return for a significant bribe. Fortunately, George and his generals learned about the plot before Arnold could deliver the fortress. Arnold escaped down the river and joined the British army, but Arnold's betrayal devastated George.

The British said that Arnold was behaving like a true patriot and gave him a command in the British army. As a result, Arnold became one of the most notorious and hated **traitors** in American history.

In May 1781, Rochambeau moved his men to meet George's force outside New York. By mid-August, George learned that the French fleet was headed toward the Chesapeake Bay in Virginia. The Americans and French would have to march more than 400 miles south. With his men weak and supplies low, George worried about the long journey. They also had to slip away from New York without alerting the British.

To trick them, George sent men to pretend to build a major camp outside New York. He spread rumors of a New York attack to British spies. The British did not suspect George's true plans until it was too late.

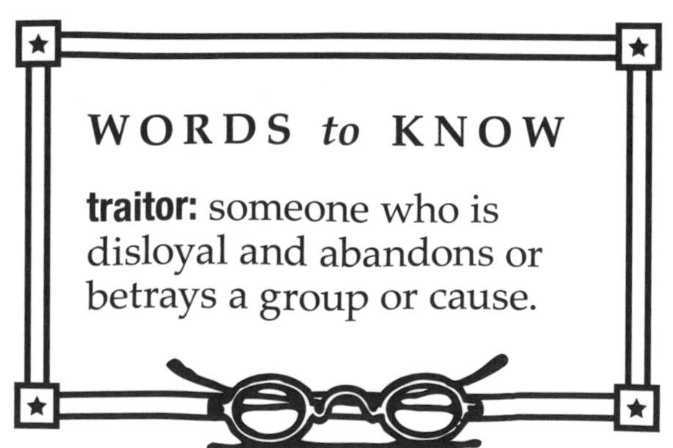

Battle of Yorktown

Meanwhile, George and Rochambeau secretly marched their men south toward Yorktown, Virginia, where the British army was encamped under the command of General Lord Charles Cornwallis. On September 2, the French fleet finally appeared off the coast of Yorktown. If Cornwallis had moved immediately, he might have escaped disaster. Believing that reinforcements were coming from the north, he decided to stay put.

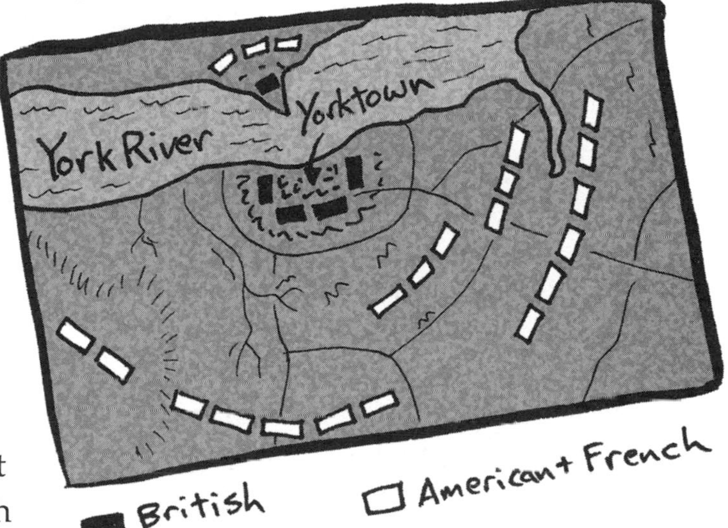

After a brief skirmish with British ships, the French fleet won control of the sea. When the Americans and French arrived on land, Cornwallis was trapped.

The battle that George had dreamed of for years was finally at hand. Rochambeau and his French troops were experts at sieges and pounded the British lines with relentless cannon fire. Realizing that help would not arrive in time, Cornwallis requested a truce to discuss surrender terms on October 17. The only other surrender George had negotiated was his own at Fort Necessity.

A Personal Loss

While George celebrated the Yorktown victory, tragedy struck. Jacky had joined him as a camp aide at Yorktown. He fell sick with camp fever and died on November 5. Martha was completely devastated by Jacky's death and needed comfort. More than ever, George was desperate for the war to end so he could return to Mount Vernon.

War's End

Although Yorktown was the last major battle of the war, minor battles and skirmishes continued for two more years. During this time, George refused to let down his guard. He insisted on keeping his army ready, drilling them constantly.

In February 1783, King George III issued a proclamation to end hostilities. On September 3, 1783, the Paris Peace Treaty officially ended the war. John Adams, Benjamin Franklin, and John Jay signed the treaty for the Americans. The treaty formally recognized the United States as a separate and independent nation.

Newburgh Conspiracy

During the war, Congress had great difficulty keeping the army supplied. Many officers had not been paid in years. They felt unappreciated by Congress and the public.

The army's unrest continued and reached a boiling point in 1783. Most of the Continental Army was camped near Newburgh, New York. Anonymous letters passed around the camp, urging the men to turn their weapons against Congress and the new nation until they were treated fairly.

On March 15, George stood before his officers and told them that any attempted coup would be against the principles for which they had fought. In his view, it would also be an attack on his honor. He pleaded with them to remain calm. Despite his passionate words, the men remained unmoved. Then George remembered that he carried a letter from a congressman in his pocket. As he opened the paper to read, he pulled out a pair of spectacles that he had never worn in public. As he adjusted the glasses, several officers began to sob at the sight of their beloved general humbled by age in front of them. By the end of the meeting, thoughts of mutiny had disappeared. It was one of George's finest moments.

IN HIS WORDS

Addressing soldiers about to mutiny in 1783

"Gentlemen, you will permit me to put on my spectacles, for I have not only grown gray, but almost blind in the service of my country."

A Commander's Farewell

After receiving word that the peace treaty had been signed, George looked forward to going home. He had been away from Mount Vernon for nearly eight years and longed for his peaceful farming routine.

George said good-bye to his soldiers in November 1783. He asked them to think of themselves as citizens of the United States first, instead of Virginians or New Englanders. At Fraunces Tavern in New York, he hugged his officers good-bye in an emotional farewell.

At a formal ceremony on December 23, 1783, in Annapolis, George officially resigned his commission. Although he had become one of the most popular and famous men in America, George vowed never to hold public office again.

George's resignation paved the way for America to grow as a free republic, not one led by a new king. When told that General Washington would return to his farm after winning the war, King George was amazed.

Did You Know?

According to European military tradition, the losing general presents his sword to the winner at the surrender ceremony. Cornwallis claimed he was too sick and he sent his second-in-command to present his sword. George called his second-in-command forward. If Cornwallis sent his second, George's second would accept.

PAST PASSAGES

"If he does that... He will be the greatest man in the world."

—KING GEORGE,
Speaking of George's decision to return to his farm

★ Make Your Own ★

Revolutionary Soldiers

1 Paint several clothespins in Revolutionary War soldiers' uniforms. The Americans wore brown or blue coats with white pants. The British wore red coats with white pants. Brown or black boots completed the look. Add details like tiny eyes, buttons, etc. Paint the stands, too.

2 Once the paint is dry, cut small strips of construction paper to make tricorn hats. Tape the edges together to join the hat sides.

3 Make several soldiers from each side so that you can set up your own battle!

SUPPLIES

- wooden clothespins, the kind without a spring
- wooden clothespin stands (optional)
- red, white, blue, black, and brown paint
- paintbrush
- construction paper
- scissors
- tape

America's First Spymaster

Not only was George Washington a farmer, general, and president, he was also America's first spymaster! When he took command of the Continental Army in 1775, he knew that the British had strong support across the colonies. British sympathizers were called Loyalists. They were eager to give the British any information that might help them. George decided to gather his own information and disrupt the British spies. He developed a network of American spies and kept their identities a closely guarded secret. He assigned each a code number so that they would not know the true identities of each other. Even George had a code number: 711. George's spies gathered information about the British. They sent messages with secret codes and invisible ink, spread false rumors, and operated under fake names.

Make Your Own

Battle Map

When planning an army's strategy, a battle map was a valuable tool. It helped generals design and coordinate troop movement, defenses, and attacks.

SUPPLIES

- paper
- black pen or marker
- tea bag
- cup of hot water

1 Using a pen or marker, draw your battle plan on a piece of paper. Make it as detailed as possible, including landmarks and geographical features like rivers, roads, and mountains. Mark your target and your current location on the map. Draw markers to show how you plan to move your troops against the enemy. Will you move as one force? Or will you divide your troops to surround the target?

2 When your battle plan is complete, dip a tea bag in a cup of hot water. It does not need to be boiling. Hot water from the kitchen sink will do. Drag the tea bag across your battle map. The tea will leave a brownish stain on the paper. Cover the entire paper with the tea stain. Set aside to dry.

3 Once the paper is dry, rip around the edges of the paper. The ripped edges and brownish tint will give your battle map an old, authentic look.

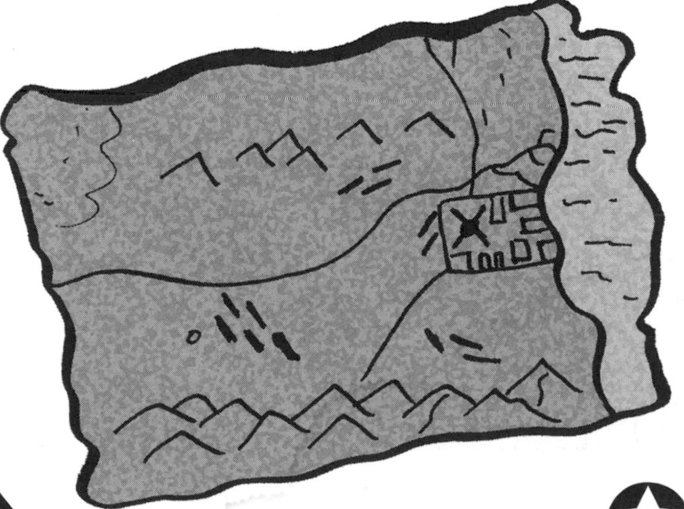

Did You Know?

During the war, a British ship sailed up the Potomac River and threatened Mount Vernon. George's cousin was managing the estate at the time and gave the British supplies in exchange for sparing the mansion. When George learned of the deal, he was extremely upset. He would rather have seen Mount Vernon burned to the ground than supply the British.

★ Make Your Own ★

Cipher Wheel

SUPPLIES

- 2 pieces of cardstock
- 2 different sized plates for tracing
- pencil
- scissors
- paper fastener
- black marker

Spies often coded secret messages during the Revolutionary War. If they were caught, the important information would not fall into enemy hands. One way to code secret messages is to use a cipher wheel.

1 Using the plates, trace two circles on your cardstock. They should be different sizes, with one at least an inch larger than the other. Cut them out, then cut a small, triangle-shaped arrow on the edge of the smaller circle.

2 Punch a hole in the center of each circle. Push the paper fastener through both holes, securing one circle on top of the other. The top circle should spin easily.

3 Starting at the top of the outer circle, write the letters of the alphabet. It's important to space them evenly around the edge of the circle. Write in pencil first so that you can erase and move them if need be. When you are satisfied with the letters, trace over them with your black marker.

4 Hold the inner circle steady and write the alphabet around the edge, mixing up the letters. Line up each letter on the inner circle with a letter on the outer circle.

5 To code your message, first write down what you want to say. Rotate the inner circle randomly. Write down the letter to which the arrow points. This is the first letter of your coded message. It will tell the person receiving the message how to position their cipher wheel.

6 Keeping your inner circle steady, find the letters of your message on the outer circle. Write down each corresponding letter from the inner circle. When you finish, your message will be coded!

7 To decode the message, your friend will need to use your cipher wheel or make an identical one. Line up the arrow so that it points to the first letter of the coded message. Find the rest of the coded letters on the inner circle and write down each matching letter on the outer circle. Read the secret message!

★ Make Your Own ★

Invisible Ink

Another way to send secret messages during the Revolutionary War was to use invisible ink.

SUPPLIES
▪ 1 lemon
▪ knife
▪ cutting board
▪ small bowl
▪ Q-tip
▪ paper
▪ electric iron

1 Place the lemon on a cutting board and cut it into two halves. Squeeze each lemon half over a small bowl, catching the lemon juice.

2 Dip a Q-tip into the lemon juice and use the wet tip to write a secret message on the paper. Watch as the wet writing disappears as it dries on the paper.

3 When you are ready to reveal your message, have an adult help you set up an electric iron. When it is hot, iron the paper with slow strokes. Make sure you do not burn the paper! As the heat from the iron hits the dried lemon juice, your secret message will be revealed!

☆ CHAPTER 6 ☆
Birth of a Nation

LEAVING POLITICS BEHIND, George enjoyed his role as a farmer again and threw himself into managing and improving his farms. Every morning, George rose early and ate a breakfast of hoecakes and tea. Then he mounted his horse and rode around the estate's farms.

Home at Last

As usual, Mount Vernon bustled with people. Jacky's two youngest children, George Washington Parke Custis and Eleanor "Nelly" Parke Custis, came to live with George and Martha. Other nieces, nephews, and relatives stayed for months at a time. The mansion's halls often rang with children's laughter.

Despite the familiar routine, the war had changed George's life. He had become a living legend. Sculptors, painters, writers, and other visitors swarmed to Mount Vernon to see and hear the famous general. He lay flat on his back as sculptors smeared plaster over his face to make **life masks**. He only put up with it because he believed it important for history's record.

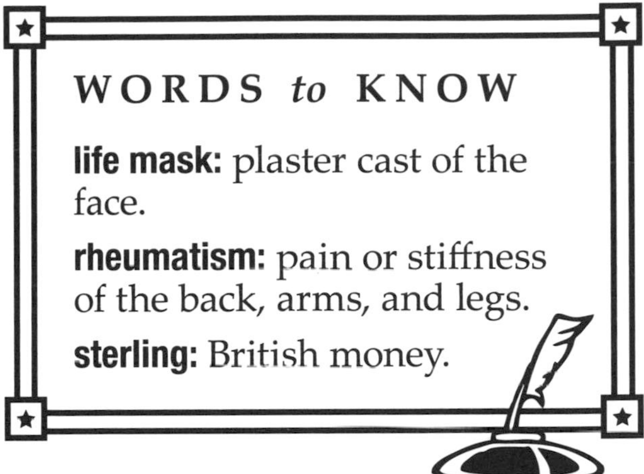

WORDS *to* KNOW

life mask: plaster cast of the face.

rheumatism: pain or stiffness of the back, arms, and legs.

sterling: British money.

During the war, George had turned 50 years old. His hair had grown gray and the skin around his eyes bore creases. His impressive figure had softened and his bones often ached with **rheumatism**. George felt his age. He planned his remaining time on earth to organize his affairs and enjoy a quiet life with family and friends.

George decided to undertake a massive project to organize his private papers for historical purposes. He hired a young officer named Richard Varick to lead the project. Varick's team worked eight hours a day for two years. At the end, they completed 28 volumes.

Business Ventures

After the war, George's finances were a complete mess. The war had cost him about 10,000 pounds **sterling**. He had paid many military expenses himself and had not taken a salary. Mount Vernon was also losing money. Since George was unwilling to sell his slaves and split up families, he owned many more slaves than he needed. The expenses of keeping the extra slaves clothed and fed drained much of the farm's profits. To bring in cash, George decided to rent or sell some of his western acres.

Constitutional Beginnings

Before the **Constitution** was created, the 13 colonies worked together under the Articles of Confederation. The Articles created an **alliance**, not a central government. Under the Articles, each state had their own freedom and independence. There were no **executive** or **judicial** branches to the central government. Instead, there was only a committee with representatives from each state. This committee was Congress.

Congress was responsible for **foreign affairs**. It could declare war and maintain an army and navy. But this power was empty because the Articles did not allow Congress to tax the states or enforce laws. This weakness showed during the war, when Congress could approve an army but could not raise money to pay for it.

In March 1786, John Jay, a member of the Continental Congress from New York, wrote to George. He said that some men in Congress wanted to revise the Articles of Confederation. In theory, George agreed. He knew the Articles would not hold the 13 colonies together much longer. However, George believed the people would resist a strong central government until a crisis changed their minds. This battle, however, was not his. In George's mind, his contribution to the new nation was complete.

WORDS *to* KNOW

constitution: a document containing the basic laws and beliefs of a country.

alliance: a group that works together for a common goal.

executive: the branch of government that carries out laws.

judicial: the branch of government that administers justice.

foreign affairs: relations with other countries.

armory: a storage place for weapons and other war equipment.

oppressive: exercising power in a cruel and unjust way.

Crisis came in the fall of 1786 when Daniel Shays, a former soldier, led 2,000 bankrupt Massachusetts farmers to protest mortgage foreclosures and taxes. They threatened the federal **armory** at Springfield. Shay's Rebellion died down, but people recognized the state's inability to stop it from happening again.

PAST PASSAGES

"Many of the members cast their eyes toward General Washington as President; and shaped their Ideas of the powers to be given to a President, by their Opinion of his Virtue."

—South Carolina delegate PIERCE BUTLER

In response to Shay's Rebellion, the states called for a convention in Philadelphia. George did not want to join the Virginia delegation, but he eventually agreed, arriving in Philadelphia in May 1787.

The delegates unanimously elected George to be president of the convention. Determined to write a new constitution instead of amending the Articles of Confederation, they debated the best way to set up the new nation's government. The government needed to be effective, but also needed safeguards against becoming **oppressive**.

PAST PASSAGES

"Be assured, his influence carried this government."

—JAMES MONROE wrote to Thomas Jefferson

As usual, George talked little while the men argued heatedly. He was still a powerful influence at the convention, though. George made his opinions quietly known through his allies, James Madison and Alexander Hamilton. The delegates looked to George when designing the government's executive branch. They allowed a strong executive office mainly because they assumed George would take the job first.

WORDS *to* KNOW

ratify: to approve formally.

checks and balances: a system of three branches of government in which no one branch becomes too powerful. Each branch can be restrained by the other two.

Throughout the summer the delegates wrote a constitution to form a central government. On September 17, they voted to accept it. Now the states had to **ratify** the Constitution. Each state would elect delegates to read, debate, and vote on the document. When 9 out of 13 states voted to approve the Constitution, it would become law.

George kept his thoughts quiet as the states debated the issues. He followed the discussions closely in newspapers and pamphlets. He felt certain that the Constitution had set up a government of the people with many **checks and balances**.

In late June 1788, word arrived of the 9th and 10th state ratifications. The Constitution was to become law.

Did You Know?

The state of Delaware is known as the First State because it was the first to ratify the Constitution; it did so on December 7, 1787.

First President

The delegates had designed the Constitution with George as the model for president. George, however, was not excited about the idea. He thought serving as president was more of a burden than an honor. Still, he knew that the young nation was fragile. It needed a strong leader to help it survive these early years. George was the one man who the entire country could rally around, just as they had done during the war. Although he did not campaign for the job, he allowed his friends to submit his name.

Did You Know?

Rhode Island was the only state that did not send representatives to the Constitutional Convention. They opposed the convention and did not want the Articles of Confederation revised.

John Adams

John Adams, the nation's first vice president, was born in Massachusetts Bay Colony in 1735. Early on, he was a leader for independence and served as a delegate to the Continental Congresses. During the war, he served as a diplomat to France and Holland. He also helped to negotiate the peace treaty.

After the war, Adams served two terms as vice president under George Washington. He found the office to be demeaning and frustrating. He wrote to his wife Abigail that "My country has in its wisdom contrived for me the most insignificant office that ever the invention of man contrived or his imagination conceived."

After Washington retired, Adams was elected the country's second president. He served only one term. Thomas Jefferson barely defeated him in 1800. A few weeks before his defeat, Adams moved into the White House in the new capital city of Washington, D.C. He was the first president to live there.

On February 4, 1789, George was elected the nation's first president. John Adams would be the vice president. On April 14 at Mount Vernon, George received the official notification of his election and accepted the job. He set out in his coach for the capital city, New York.

As George traveled, people came out to show their support of him. Thousands gathered and cheered between cannon salutes and tributes. Cities held parades and dinners. Although he appreciated the support, George sometimes called the whole affair painful.

George had doubts about his ability to serve as president. He wondered if his age would hurt him. He feared failure and the loss of his hard-earned reputation.

He told Henry Knox, "My movement to the Chair of Government will be accompanied by feelings not unlike those of a culprit who is going to the place of his execution."

Despite his doubts, George stood on the balcony of Federal Hall on April 30, 1789, and took the oath of office. Once again, he would lead the nation.

Letter Writing

In colonial America, there were no telephones or email messages. Instead, people wrote letters to communicate. Because paper was often scarce, colonial men and women filled every inch of a page with writing. Once the letter was finished, they did not go to a mailbox or post office to send the letter. The letter was passed from hand to hand as colonists traveled until it finally reached the person for whom it was written. In some cases, this could take months!

Then & Now

Make Your Own

Purple Heart Medal

SUPPLIES

- purple felt or fabric
- scissors
- lace to edge all sides of the heart
- needle
- thread
- safety pin

1 Cut a heart from the purple felt or fabric. Sew the lace around the edges of the heart using a needle and thread.

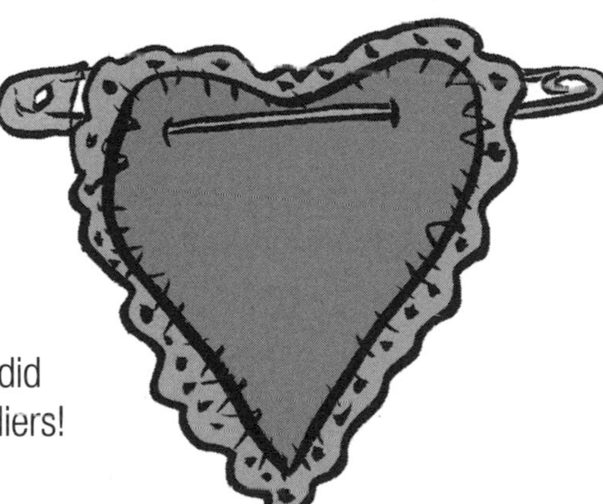

2 Using a safety pin, pin the Purple Heart medal over your left breast, just as George did for the Continental soldiers!

Purple Heart

While at Newburgh, George designed the Purple Heart badge. It was to be awarded for a singular act of merit. The original badge was a heart cut from purple cloth and edged with narrow silver lace. It was to be worn over the left breast on the uniform. Awardees' names would be recorded in a Book of Merit.

George awarded the Purple Heart three times. Connecticut sergeants Elijah Churchill, William Brown, and Daniel Bissell, Jr., received the Purple Heart during the Revolutionary War.

No other soldier received the Purple Heart until 1932. To honor George's 200th birthday, the Purple Heart was redesigned to include George's picture in the center.

★ Make Your Own ★

Letter Seal

In the eighteenth century, people sealed letters by melting wax onto the paper. Sometimes they pressed a seal into the hot wax to leave a distinctive pattern. Ask an adult to help you with the candle and matches in this project.

SUPPLIES

- 1 cup cornstarch
- 2 cups baking soda
- 1¼ cups water
- saucepan
- spoon
- stove
- wax paper
- food coloring (optional)
- kitchen towel
- ziptop bag
- folded letter or paper
- candle
- match

1 Mix cornstarch, baking soda, and water in a saucepan. Cook the mixture over medium heat, stirring regularly. Be patient, it may take a few minutes! The mixture will stiffen into a clay-like consistency.

2 Spoon the clay onto a large piece of wax paper. Be careful, it will be hot! When the clay has cooled enough to touch, knead it until smooth. If you want, add a few drops of food coloring and knead some more.

3 Roll a small piece of clay into a tube shape about 3 inches long and 1 inch wide. Slowly press one end against a hard surface to spread it wider than the rest of the tube.

4 Choose a letter of the alphabet for your seal. Roll a thin strip of clay and form the letter. The letter needs to be backwards so it reads properly in the wax.

5 Gently press the letter onto the base of the tube, being careful not to flatten the letter. You now have a seal with a raised backwards letter on its base.

6 Let the clay harden for at least 24 hours. Wrap any leftover clay in a damp kitchen towel and store it in a ziptop bag. You may want to use the clay for the clay bust project in Chapter 8!

7 Once the clay has hardened, fold a letter in thirds. Light the candle and carefully drip wax where the paper sides meet. Keep dripping until you have formed a solid wax circle about 1 inch wide. Before the wax hardens, firmly press your letter seal into the wax.

★ Make Your Own ★

George Washington Wig

In the 1700s, many men wore wigs as a fashion statement. The wigs were made of human, horse, goat, or yak hair and were often powdered white.

SUPPLIES

- newspaper
- brown paper grocery bag
- pencil
- scissors
- tape
- white paint
- paintbrush
- cotton balls
- glue
- ribbon

1 Cover your work surface with newspaper. Place the brown paper bag over your head. Have someone draw an outline of your forehead, reaching around your ears and down to your neck and shoulders.

2 Cut along the pencil line to create the wig's base. Trim the bag if necessary to adjust the fit. You can make folds in the sides and tape them to make the base fit your head better.

3 Paint the bag white. When the paint has dried, glue cotton balls on the bag. Completely cover the surface, making the balls touch each other.

4 Tie a piece of ribbon into a bow. Glue the bow to the back of the wig near the nape of the neck. Put your wig on and pretend to be George Washington!

✰ CHAPTER 7 ✰
Washington's Presidency

AS THE NATION'S FIRST PRESIDENT, George realized that everything he did would be studied and copied by future presidents. The task before him was enormous. The states were not united. There were about 4 million people spread along the coast and moving west. Many felt little allegiance to the newly created United States. Some were only loyal to themselves. Others gave their loyalty to state, local, or regional governments. Many believed that uniting so many people over so great a distance was an impossible task. They waited for the new government to fail.

Illness

One of George's first challenges, however, was not political. Instead, his own body waged war against him. In June 1789, a large tumor appeared on his left thigh. After surgeons removed the tumor, George's condition was critical for a few days. Then in May 1790, he hovered near death with the flu. His aging body healed slowly and recovery from the illnesses took a long time. He was no longer the young man who had led the army.

IN HIS WORDS

About his presidency

"I walk on untrodden ground. There is scarcely any part of my conduct which may not hereafter be drawn into **precedent**."

Gathering Advisors

Throughout his life, George had gathered bright and talented men to his side and sought their advice. As president he surrounded himself with one of the greatest groups of statesmen in American history. James Madison became George's **liaison** with Congress. Thomas Jefferson was his **secretary of state**. Alexander Hamilton led the treasury. Henry Knox took command as secretary of war and John Jay headed the judicial branch.

One man often absent from **cabinet** meetings was John Adams. Although Congress had elected John Adams as vice president, George and Adams were not close. George rarely consulted with Adams or invited him to his cabinet meetings. For his part, Adams kept busy with the congress, the legislative branch of government that made the laws. He was often jealous and critical of George.

Did You Know?

George often preferred to bow in greeting instead of shaking hands. Some said that was proof of his snobbery. Others point out that George had enormous and powerful hands. They claim he may have bowed to avoid crushing the hands of his guests!

WORDS *to* KNOW

precedent: a decision that serves as a guide for the future.

liaison: link or connection.

secretary of state: the person in charge of foreign affairs.

cabinet: a government leader's group of advisors.

Bill of Rights

One of the first things George did as president was ask James Madison to create a bill of rights that would protect the people's freedom. This was something that was missing from the Constitution.

Madison wrote 10 amendments to the Constitution. The first amendment promised the freedom of religion for all citizens. Other amendments guaranteed the right to free speech, the right to bear arms, and protection from unlawful search and seizure. Together, the 10 amendments would become known as the Bill of Rights. The bill passed quickly through Congress. After being ratified by the states, it became law on December 15, 1791.

Hamilton's War Debt Solution

When George took office, he discovered that the country's finances were a complete disaster. The country had borrowed a large amount of money to pay for the war.

PAST PASSAGES

"Learn to think continentally."

—ALEXANDER HAMILTON

George handed the entire mess over to Alexander Hamilton, his secretary of the treasury. Hamilton was a financial genius and the right man for the task. He dove into the numbers immediately. Three months later, he presented a report showed that the country was in debt for $77.1 million.

Hamilton proposed a plan to keep the enormous debt from strangling the young country. Part of the plan was to consolidate all the war debt. Hamilton wanted to create a national bank that would take over the states' unpaid war debts. The bank would manage the country's investments and payments at a national level.

Congress hotly argued Hamilton's plan. Some men, like James Madison, feared that debt consolidation and a national bank was getting too close to a monarchy. Taking over the state debt was also bitterly argued. States like Virginia who had already paid their war debts felt it was unfair that other states like Massachusetts would get theirs paid by the federal government. Hamilton was firm in his response. It was important to get rid of the country's war debt once and for all. The country needed a fresh start with good money and credit.

George remained silent throughout the uproar. Although he supported Hamilton's plan, he did not interfere with the congressional debates. Eventually, Hamilton's financial plan was approved.

Thomas Jefferson

Thomas Jefferson was one of the most influential men during the formation of the country. Born in Virginia on April 13, 1743, Jefferson studied at the College of William and Mary in Williamsburg. After college, he practiced law and joined the Virginia House of Burgesses.

In 1776, Jefferson served as one of Virginia's delegates to the Continental Congress and wrote the Declaration of Independence. Its signing on July 4, 1776, became the birthday of the United States.

After the United States won its freedom from Britain, Jefferson served as secretary of state in President Washington's administration. He was a firm defender of state rights, opposed a centralized government, and had many clashes over politics with another presidential advisor, Alexander Hamilton. Jefferson resigned from Washington's cabinet in 1793.

He returned to public service as vice president in 1796 and was elected the nation's third president in 1800. As president, one of Jefferson's greatest legacies was the Louisiana Purchase. He bought the large parcel of land called the Louisiana Territory from Napoleon Bonaparte, leader of France, in 1803. After completing his second term as president in 1809, Jefferson retired to Monticello, his home in Virginia. He died there on the 50th birthday of the nation, July 4, 1826.

Hamilton's complex plan was a success. George was able to run the government without worrying about a crushing debt. Within 20 years, only 25 percent of the debt remained. America's credit was restored around the world.

Capital City

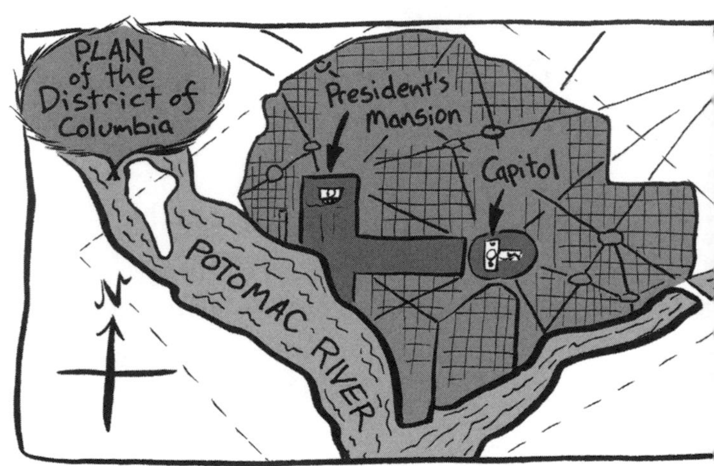

The Constitution called for Congress to build a capital city. Each state argued for the capital to be close to their region. One congressman became so frustrated at the endless arguing, he suggested that the new capital should be put on wheels and rolled from state to state.

Eventually, a site was chosen on the Potomac River. Thomas Jefferson feared that if Congress took responsibility, the city might never be built. He proposed having the president manage the city's development. Congress agreed and handed George control of the capital.

George took over the capital city's design with the same attention that he gave his own home. He selected a site on the Potomac not far from Mount Vernon. He appointed commissioners and hired architects. He approved a plan for a tract of land that spread over almost 10 square miles. George also approved the design of the presidential mansion and the Capitol building. While construction was in progress, he reviewed regular reports and visited the site to monitor its progress.

Did You Know?

Although George helped design the new American capital that bore his name, he would never live in it.

Retirement Plans

As George's first term neared its end, he felt he had done a good job. He also believed it was important for him to retire voluntarily. That way he could peacefully pass leadership to the next elected official. If he died in office, the presidency would pass to the vice president without an election. It would be too similar to a king's throne passing to his son.

At 60, George felt his mind and body growing old. His memory was becoming worse and he could not physically keep up with activities he had once enjoyed. He told his cabinet that he was not running for a second term and asked Madison to help him draft a farewell address. It was time to go home.

Foreign Policy and Indian Affairs

Across the ocean, France struggled in its own revolution. George watched with interest but firmly believed that the United States should avoid being dragged into European affairs at all costs. The United States was not strong enough for another war.

George was convinced that America's future lay to the west, in the land that George had explored as a young man. Native Americans lived on that land. They were strong fighters who were not happy about white settlers invading their lands. George wanted to create an agreement with them that would allow peaceful settlement of the western lands.

George and advisor Henry Knox designed a plan to create several Native American homelands in the western territory. Unfortunately, there was too much conflict over the land for George's plan to become more than a distant hope.

Trouble in the Cabinet and a Second Term

As George planned his retirement, hostilities grew between two cabinet members. Thomas Jefferson and Alexander Hamilton had disagreed on policy for years. Hamilton, a **Federalist**, believed in a stronger federal government. Jefferson, however, feared that attempts to strengthen and consolidate government would lead the country to **monarchy**. A **Republican**, he favored stronger state control. George understood both positions and tried to walk a moderate path.

The divide between Federalists and Republicans grew in the public as well. Both sides used the press to promote their views and attack the other side. Republicans were becoming more critical of George's administration. They believed it leaned too far to the Federalist side. Although they often stopped short of attacking George himself, others in the government were fair game.

"North and South will hang together, only if they have you to hang on."

—THOMAS JEFFERSON to George, regarding retirement

PAST PASSAGES

Over time, Jefferson and Hamilton's political disagreements became personal. The two men hated each other and engaged in bitter attacks. The only thing they could agree on was that George should stay for a second term.

WORDS *to* KNOW

Federalist: a political party in the late 1700s that favored a strong central government.

monarchy: rule by a king.

Republican: a political party in the late 1700s that supported state rights.

George discretely asked if there was anyone else considered for president. There was no one. Discouraged, George wondered how he could leave office. He could not ignore that signs pointed to a growing political crisis. The split in his cabinet and the increasing divide between Federalists and Republicans troubled him. The country needed his steady hand once again.

With a heavy heart, George put aside his farewell address. On February 13, 1793, he was elected to a second term, with Adams as his vice president again. On March 4, 1793, George rode in his carriage through the streets of Philadelphia, the new capital, to his inauguration. After his speech, he returned to the presidential mansion. He did not feel like celebrating.

War in Europe

Foreign affairs would be the focus of George's second term. The French Revolution took a bloody turn as the new government beheaded King Louis XVI and declared a new French republic. George recognized the new government, even if he disagreed with their violence. They were breaking free of monarchy, just as the United States had done a few years earlier.

In April 1793, George received word that France had declared war on Britain. The two European powers tried to bring the Americans into the conflict. The British still controlled the sea and seized American ships as they sailed to France. The British also still held several forts on the United States frontier and used them to encourage Native American resistance to the Americans.

The French, on the other hand, believed that the Americans owed them allegiance after their support of the American Revolution. They were brothers in a similar cause. If the United States government did not come to France's side, the French believed the American people would rally for France. They wanted to use American ports and sailors to equip **privateers** to raid British trade ships.

George believed that the United States could not afford to be drawn into the conflict. Remaining out of the fight was in America's long-term best interests. Ten days after learning about the war, he released a Proclamation of **Neutrality**.

Did You Know?

The political differences between Hamilton and Jefferson were the beginnings of the American two-party political system. Most see this as one of the greatest contributions of the Founding Fathers. At the time, though, they viewed it as a curse.

In 1793, France's revolutionary cause was popular with Americans. They demonstrated on the streets and demanded that the United States declare war on Britain. Jefferson and his Republican allies led the calls to support France. They argued that by remaining neutral, the United States was actually helping the British.

The newspapers reflected the country's pro-French feelings. They attacked George's administration and neutral position. They also began to attack George personally. These attacks on his character greatly upset George.

Nevertheless, George remained firm in his conviction to stay out of the war. What was happening in France made him uneasy. He feared that revolutionary **fervor** would crumble into chaos. Although Jefferson and the Republicans laughed at George's dire predictions, they would soon come true. During 1793 and 1794, France descended into the **Reign of Terror**. The new government beheaded thousands of people on the **guillotine**.

WORDS *to* KNOW

privateer: an armed ship that is privately owned but hired by a government to fight enemy ships.

neutrality: policy of not getting involved in a war between other countries.

fervor: great feeling.

Reign of Terror: a period of time during the French Revolution, from 1793 to 1794, when many people were killed by the ruling group.

guillotine: a device that uses a heavy blade positioned between two posts to cut off a person's head.

IN HIS WORDS

About attacks on his character

"I would rather be on my farm than to be made emperor of the world and yet I am being charged with wanting to be a king!"

As the attacks between the Republicans and the Federalists grew, Jefferson decided to resign as secretary of state. He told George that he was tired of public life and needed to attend to his affairs at home. George unsuccessfully tried to convince him to stay. Jefferson's departure would leave George's cabinet unbalanced. Without him, there was no strong Republican voice to offset Hamilton's Federalist views. Although he delayed his departure until the end of 1793, Jefferson could not be swayed.

To complicate matters, hostilities with England soon flared when British ships started seizing American ships sailing to the French West Indies. Anti-British feelings exploded across the country. To resolve the problem, George sent Chief Justice John Jay to London to negotiate.

The Whiskey Rebellion

George then turned his attention to issues at home. One particular problem involved a group of western Pennsylvania farmers. These farmers used grain to distill whiskey, which they sold. They were angered by a tax on whiskey. By placing a tax on the liquor, the government took away their profits. To them, the whiskey tax was just as bad as the Stamp Act had been for their fathers. Many refused to pay.

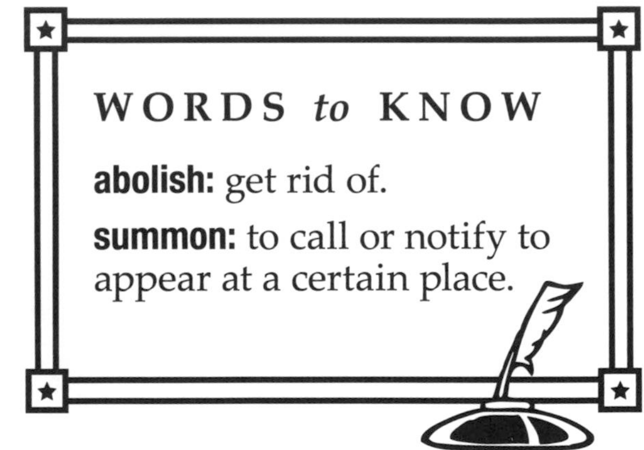

WHAT IF? The Constitution Freed the Slaves

In hindsight, one of George's greatest failings was that he never found a way to end slavery. By the end of the Revolutionary War, George was already personally opposed to slavery and convinced that freeing of the slaves was in the best interest of the country. The South used slaves for tobacco planting, but had not yet become reliant on slave labor for cotton plantations. A small window of opportunity existed to **abolish** slavery.

As the Constitution was being drafted, George feared that if slavery entered the debate, the southern states would not ratify the Constitution. In the end, George and the other Founding Fathers decided that it was more important to get the Constitution passed and ratified than to make a dramatic stand about slavery. The Constitution passed and the country missed a great opportunity to end slavery. The path to civil war was set.

In July 1794, federal officers tried to **summon** 60 tax evaders before a Philadelphia court. In response, a group of armed men rioted and burned the home of the head tax collector. They gathered near Pittsburgh and taunted the government. Some mobs branded government officials with hot irons. George authorized a federal force of 13,000 men from several state militias and led the men across Pennsylvania.

The rebellion fell apart as George's force approached. George explained his actions to Congress by saying that citizens had the right to disagree with the government and voice their views. They did not, however, have the right to violate federal law. Congress agreed and congratulated George for defending the Constitution.

The Jay Treaty

In early 1795, John Jay and the British government drew up a treaty. The British agreed to turn over their northwestern forts to the Americans. The treaty increased trade between the two countries. Although the treaty avoided war with Britain, George was not happy with everything in it.

He realized the treaty would anger Republicans. Jay had agreed to allow the British to continue seizing American ships headed to France and her holdings. In addition, for 15 years American ships could not carry goods to England that would compete with those produced in the British West Indies. This included cotton, one of the South's growing exports. The Republicans would claim the treaty openly favored Britain.

Did You Know?

The Whiskey Rebellion was the first and last time that a sitting president would lead troops in the field.

Did You Know?

At first, George insisted that he would not take a salary, as he had done in the Revolutionary War. When Congress refused, George eventually agreed to a salary of $25,000 per year, which was a lot of money in 1789.

As news of the unpopular treaty's terms spread, the public's anger erupted. Mobs burned mock images of Jay. They also turned on George. The newspapers ran personal attacks on his character and his career. In this atmosphere, George prepared to give his seventh annual address to the Congress. As he walked into the Senate on December 8, 1795, the air was filled with tension. Many wondered how the old general would defend himself now.

As George began to speak, he reminded the assembled men of the country's recent successes. He pointed out that the country was prosperous and growing. To the Republicans' amazement, George had once again deftly outmaneuvered his critics and turned the situation in his favor.

IN HIS WORDS

Speaking to Congress

"Is it too much to say that our country exhibits a spectacle of national happiness never before surpassed if ever equaled?"

Painful Attacks

The personal attacks over the Jay Treaty wounded George deeply. The betrayal of Thomas Jefferson, however, hit even harder. As secretary of state, Jefferson had often supported George in public, and then quietly spoken against him to Republicans.

Several people had warned George about Jefferson's two-faced politics, but George would hear nothing of it. Despite their political differences, George trusted Jefferson. When told that Jefferson was calling him "quasi-senile" in private letters, George chose not to believe it.

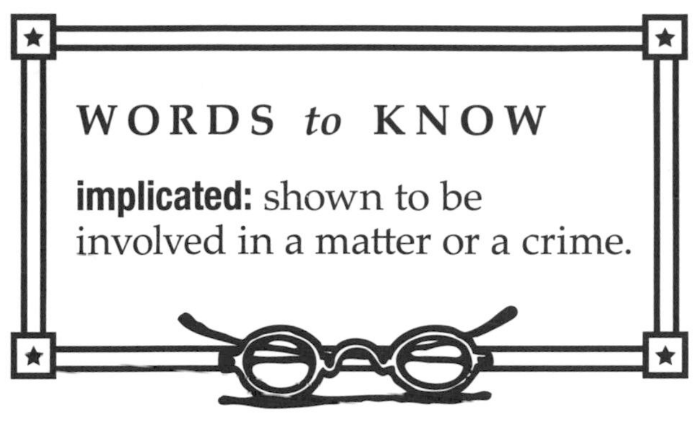

WORDS *to* KNOW

implicated: shown to be involved in a matter or a crime.

Jefferson, however, was a key figure behind the Republican attacks on George's presidency. He took special care to make sure he was not **implicated** in any of the press documents. But by July 1796, George could no longer ignore the truth. Jefferson was running a smear campaign behind his back. He wrote to Jefferson about a recent list of accusations. After another of Jefferson's private letters against George appeared in the papers the following year, all correspondence between the two men stopped.

After the bitterness and controversy of his second term, George was heartily sick of politics and the presidency. With firm resolve, he sat down to write his farewell address.

★ Make Your Own ★

Colonial Flag

The first official United States flag was adopted by an act of Congress on June 14, 1777. A group led by George had designed the flag and hired Betsy Ross to create it. Originally they asked for 13 stars that were 6-pointed. When Betsy showed them how she could cut perfect, five-pointed stars with just one snip of the scissors, they agreed to stars with five points.

SUPPLIES

- picture of American flag with 13 stars and 13 stripes
- ruler
- red, white, and blue felt
- scissors
- glue

1. Start with a piece of red felt about 9 inches by 11½ inches.
2. From the white felt, cut six stripes about a half inch wide and 11½ inches long.
3. Cut a square from the blue felt approximately 5 inches wide and 4 inches tall. Cut out 13 white stars.
4. Assemble your flag first, without gluing. Once everything is in position, glue the felt stars and stripes to the flag.

✰ CHAPTER 8 ✰

Washington's Farewell

AS GEORGE PREPARED TO RESIGN, he turned to his old advisor Alexander Hamilton for help in writing his farewell address. The address announced his decision to retire after 45 years of serving America. It would be his last and greatest farewell.

Philadelphia's *American Daily Advisor* published George's farewell address on September 19, 1796. Newspapers around the country reprinted the address so that citizens in every state could read George's words.

George's parting address has become one of the most important historical documents of the United States. In it, he gave his final advice to the nation. At its core, the address stressed the importance of being united at home.

IN HIS WORDS

Speaking to Congress

"The Unity of Government which constitutes you one people is also now dear to you. It is justly so; for it is a main Pillar in the **Edifice** of your real independence, the support of your **tranquility** at home; your peace abroad; of your safety; of your prosperity; of that very Liberty which you so highly prize."

He also warned against letting political differences divide the nation and stressed the importance of religion, **morality**, and avoiding debt.

In his farewell, George reminded the people, "The name of AMERICAN, which belongs to you, in your national capacity, must always exalt the just pride of Patriotism . . . You have in a common cause fought and **triumphed** together." It was a grand finale to his public career.

Final Days in Office

George spent his last days in office winding down his business. He gave his final speech to Congress on December 7, 1796. He sent more instructions to the builders of the new capital city. He and Martha also packed and prepared to move back to Mount Vernon.

During the next presidential election, George did not publicly speak for any candidate. After a close vote, the country elected John Adams as president and Thomas Jefferson as vice president.

WORDS *to* KNOW

edifice: a large, impressive building or organization.

tranquility: calmness and peacefulness.

morality: conforming to rules of conduct.

triumph: victory.

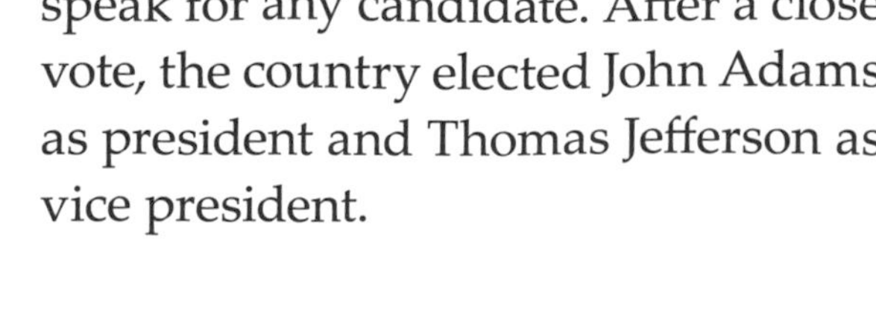

Dances and dinners in his honor filled George's last days in office. The ceremonies continued until Adams' inauguration. It irritated Adams when he noticed that many people paid more attention to George than to him on inauguration day. At the ceremony, George appeared relaxed and happy. Adams told his wife later that he thought he heard George muttering at the ceremony's end, "Ay! I am fairly out and you fairly in! See which of us will be the happiest!"

IN HIS WORDS

About foreign affairs

"Europe has a set of primary interests, which to us have none, or a very remote relation . . . 'Tis our true policy to steer clear of permanent Alliances, with any portion of the foreign world."

Return Home

A few days after Adams' inauguration, George and Martha left for Mount Vernon. They shipped many of their possessions and packed the rest into the family carriage. "On one side, I am called upon to remember the parrot; on the other, to remember the dog. For my own part, I should not pine if they were both forgot," George joked. On March 15, 1797, the carriage pulled into Mount Vernon's driveway. George was home at last.

He soon discovered that the years he spent taking care of the nation had taken their toll on his estate. The house and barns needed repair. The fields were a shambles. Even the horses, sheep, and cows had become weaker and smaller without his careful breeding. George hired painters and carpenters to make the repairs. Soon, the smell of paint and the noise of hammers filled the house.

Daily visitors streamed into Mount Vernon. Some were friends and **colleagues**. Others were simply strangers who came to get a glimpse of the great man. Virginia hospitality would not let the Washingtons turn anyone away. At one point, George was shocked to realize that he and Martha had not eaten alone in more than 20 years! Despite the flow of guests, George was lonely. Many of his close friends, such as the Fairfaxes, had moved away or died.

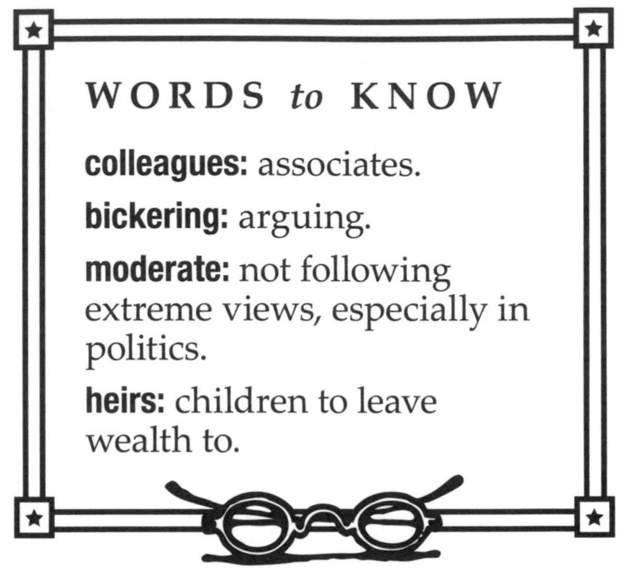

WORDS *to* KNOW

colleagues: associates.

bickering: arguing.

moderate: not following extreme views, especially in politics.

heirs: children to leave wealth to.

With the estate in disrepair, George needed money. He sold pieces of his western land holdings, but still refused to sell his slaves.

Politics Intrude

Even in his retirement, George followed events at home and in Europe. While in office, George had tried to remain above party **bickering**. He listened to Federalist and Republican positions, then chose his own **moderate** path. At home, however, he became more Federalist in his beliefs. He also grew angry with French attacks on American ships. He suspected that the pro-French Republicans might cooperate if the French invaded America.

IN HIS WORDS

Declining a third term

"The vessel is afloat or very nearly so, and considering myself as a passenger only, I shall trust to the mariners whose duty it is to watch, to steer into a safe port."

Did You Know?

The Constitution did not limit how long a president could serve. By ending his presidency after two terms, George set an important precedent for future leaders.

When France refused to accept three American diplomats without a bribe, President Adams authorized an increase of troops. Without asking, Adams appointed George commander in chief once again. In November 1798, George traveled to Philadelphia to work on plans for the new army. Fortunately, the French crisis faded and the army was not needed.

In July 1799, George received a letter from Governor Trumbull of Connecticut. Trumbull pleaded with the old statesman to consider the presidency one more time. This time, George firmly declined. The steering of the country was no longer George's responsibility.

Last Will and Testament

George was busy settling his affairs and writing his will. With no **heirs**, George spread his holdings between more than 20 relatives. To friends and faithful servants, he left cash gifts and special items like his desk, chair, and spyglass. He donated money to create a national university in the new capital city.

George also picked his burial spot. He did not want a national burial with a parade and ceremony. Instead, he asked for a private burial at Mount Vernon. Not far from the house, he marked an area that had a view of the land and river. In his will, he instructed that a brick tomb should be built there. It should not be too grand, but large enough to hold other family members if they wished.

Also in his will, George tackled slavery. The issue had haunted him for years. During the war, he was at first shocked by free blacks in the New England army. Soon, however, he became used to his **integrated** army and even urged the South to promise freedom to slaves who enlisted.

George came to see his dependence on slaves at Mount Vernon as a misfortune. Still, he was conflicted on how to resolve the problem. Mount Vernon could not operate without slave labor and, at the time, there was no free labor available in Virginia.

WORDS *to* KNOW

integrated: including members of different races, religions, and backgrounds.

pension: a fixed amount of money paid on regular intervals to older workers.

Sometime in 1793, however, George reached a conclusion. He planned to rent his farms, except the mansion house farms, to expert English farmers. When he freed the slaves, George would encourage the English renters to hire them back as free workers.

Did You Know?

George's plan to free his slaves would mean a tremendous financial sacrifice on his part. He would be giving up one of his largest financial assets. In addition, he planned to support the freed slave children until they were adults and give a **pension** *to slaves who were too old or sick to work.*

When he created a list of his slaves, a problem arose. For years, George had encouraged his slaves to marry. Now, as he wanted to free them, those marriages complicated matters. George could only legally free the slaves he owned outright. The others were part of the Custis estate. Upon Martha's death, they belonged to her grandchildren and George had no legal right to free them. If he freed his half, it would break up the slave families. Unable to find a practical solution, George put off the decision until he wrote his will.

IN HIS WORDS

In his will regarding his slaves

"Upon the decease of my wife, it is my Will and desire, that all the slaves which I hold in my own right, shall receive their freedom."

His wish for freedom for all of his slaves came true about a year after his death when Martha freed the remaining slaves. After granting them freedom, George's estate supported these people for more than 30 years. George had hoped that he would set an example for other Americans and Southerners. He was the only Founding Father to do so.

A Hero Dies

On December 12, 1799, a gray and cloudy morning dawned. Snow, hail, and cold rain fell. Despite the weather, George insisted on his usual routine of riding for several hours. When he returned, snow clung to his hair and his neck was wet.

The next day George developed a sore throat. He refused any medicine, saying that he had caught a cold and it would pass. During the night, however, George woke Martha. He was having difficulty breathing, but he insisted that Martha wait until morning to call a doctor.

Colonial Medicine

During George Washington's time, many people couldn't afford a doctor. They treated themselves with herbal or animal remedies. A common treatment used when a doctor was called was bleeding, which was done by piercing a vein, cutting the skin, or applying leeches. Colonial doctors believed that releasing poisoned blood would help a person recover faster from an infection. Unfortunately, bleeding often had the opposite effect and made the patient grow sicker or die from loss of blood.

Then & Now

On December 14, George's long-time friend Dr. Craik arrived. He and two other doctors tried several **remedies** to ease George's illness. They bled him four different times, a common medical treatment believed to clean infected blood, and had him gargle sage tea and vinegar. The doctors urged him to cough and gave George medicines to make him vomit. Despite their efforts, George's condition did not improve.

As the afternoon passed, George became convinced that this day would be his last. He called for Martha and told her where to find his will. Barely able to speak through his swollen throat, George asked his secretary Tobias Lear if his papers and affairs were in order.

Martha in Mourning

In her grief, Martha did not attend George's funeral. She abandoned the bedroom where she and George had spent their 50-year marriage. Instead, she moved into a small room on the mansion's third floor. After George's death, Martha destroyed their private letters to each other. It was her decision to keep their personal life away from the prying eyes of history. She would not live long without George, and died three years later, in 1802.

That evening, George's breathing grew more difficult. In a low voice, he repeatedly asked what time it was. To Dr. Craik, he said, "I die hard, but I am not afraid to go . . ." Throughout his suffering, George did not complain. He thanked his doctors and asked that they do no more.

As the night grew dark, the fear of being buried alive came over George. He instructed Lear that his body should be placed in the burial vault no less than three days after his death. Lear nodded yes.

WHAT IF? Antibiotics Existed in the Eighteenth Century

Modern doctors agree that George most likely died of an infection in his throat. A simple dose of antibiotics probably would have saved George's life. However, this kind of medication was not available in the eighteenth century. Had he lived, the story of George's life may have had new and interesting chapters.

"'Tis well," murmured George. These are believed to be his last words. Sometime before midnight, George Washington died. He was 67 years old.

WORDS *to* KNOW

remedy: a healing medicine or treatment.

eulogy: a speech or writing in honor of a dead person.

A Nation in Mourning

Four days later, George was buried in the family vault. News of George's death spread throughout the country. Grief poured out over the loss of the old commander and statesman. Newspapers published tributes. In Congress, state legislatures, and town meetings, men expressed their sorrow. Across the country, people staged funeral processions and held **eulogies**.

Great speakers remembered their hero. At the House of Representatives, Henry Lee famously spoke of his friend:

"First in war—first in peace—and first in the hearts of his countrymen, his example was as **edifying** to all around him as were the effects of that example lasting...Such was the man for whom our nation mourns...he was second to none in the humble and endearing scenes of private life: pious, just, humane, temperate, and sincere; uniform, dignified, and commanding..."

—HENRY LEE

PAST PASSAGES

More than any other person, George Washington was the symbol of America's government of the people. He was a wise, caring, and selfless man who stepped forward to serve at the most critical moments. Without his steady hand and guidance, 13 separate colonies may never have grown into one of the world's greatest and most prosperous nations. For all time, George Washington will be remembered as America's first national hero.

Did You Know?

In February 1790, the practice of celebrating George Washington's birthday as a national holiday became a tradition.

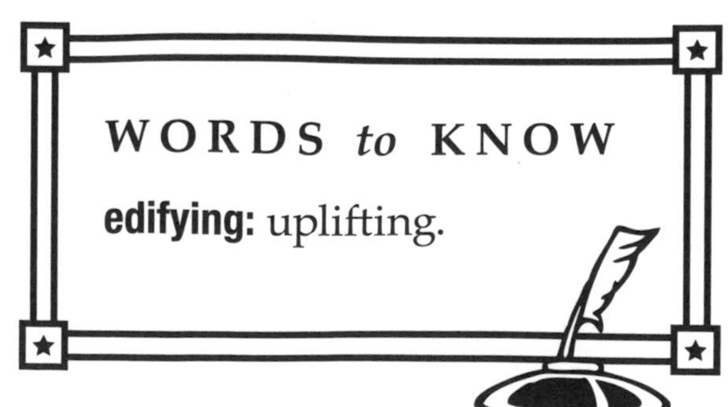

WORDS *to* KNOW

edifying: uplifting.

Make Your Own

Silhouette Art

In the 1700s, silhouettes were popular pieces of art. A silhouette is an outline filled in with a dark color, on a light background.

SUPPLIES

- large sheet of white paper
- tape
- volunteer
- chair
- lamp or bright light
- pencil
- scissors
- large piece of black paper
- large piece of colored or white paper
- glue

1. Find a volunteer to sit for a silhouette portrait. Tape a large piece of white paper to the wall and have your volunteer sit in front of it, sideways to the wall.
2. Shine a bright light at the wall to cast your volunteer's shadow on the white paper. Experiment with moving the light to see where you get the clearest shadow.
3. Trace your volunteer's profile onto the white paper. Cut out the profile and tape it onto a piece of black paper. Trace and cut the silhouette from the black paper.
4. To create your silhouette art, glue the black profile against a piece of white or colored paper. The silhouette is ready to display!

Did You Know?

George's doctors measured him carefully for a lined mahogany coffin. They recorded that he was 6 feet 3½ inches tall at the time of his death.

★ Make Your Own ★

Clay Bust

As George's fame grew, he spent many hours posing for artists and sculptors. Pretend you are a famous artist creating your own sculpture of George!

SUPPLIES

- 1 cup cornstarch
- 2 cups baking soda
- 1¼ cups water
- saucepan
- stove
- spoon
- wax paper
- food coloring (optional)
- kitchen towel
- ziptop bag
- paint and brush

1. Mix cornstarch, baking soda, and water in a saucepan. Cook the mixture over medium heat, stirring regularly. Be patient, it may take a few minutes! The mixture will stiffen into a clay-like consistency.

2. Spoon the clay onto a large piece of wax paper. Be careful, it will be hot! When the clay has cooled enough to touch, knead it until smooth. If you want to color the clay, add a few drops of food coloring and knead until well mixed.

3. To make your clay bust, roll a small ball to form George's head. Next, create a base or shoulder area for the ball to rest on, complete with clothing.

4. Add details like eyes, nose, and mouth to the face. To create hair, roll thin ropes of clay and drape the ropes across the forehead like the outline of hair. Add more ropes to fill out the head. Bending and waving the ropes will give the look of curly hair. Make sure you leave the ropes in the back long enough to pull into a ponytail, or cue.

5. If you want, you can paint the bust after the clay has dried. Wrap any remaining clay in a damp kitchen towel and store in a ziptop bag. You may want to use the extra clay for the letter seal project!

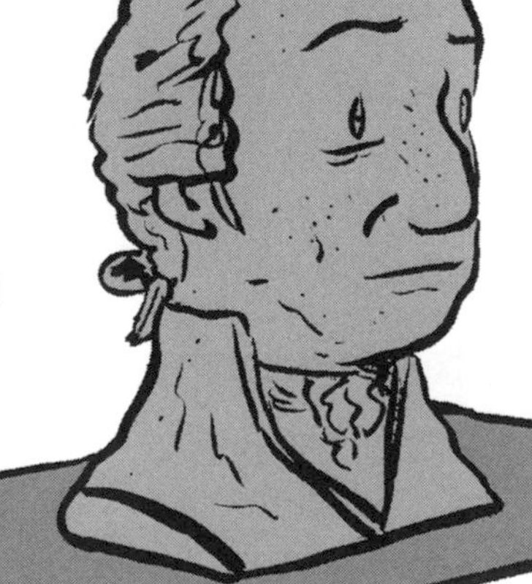

Washington Monument

SUPPLIES

- picture of the Washington Monument
- empty cereal box
- scissors
- pencil
- ruler
- white, gray, or silver paint
- paintbrush
- tape

The Washington Monument is a 555-foot-tall obelisk in Washington, D.C. It is made of marble, granite, and sandstone. The monument is one of the world's tallest stone structure and the world's tallest obelisk. An obelisk is a tall stone pillar with a square base and sides that taper to a point like a pyramid.

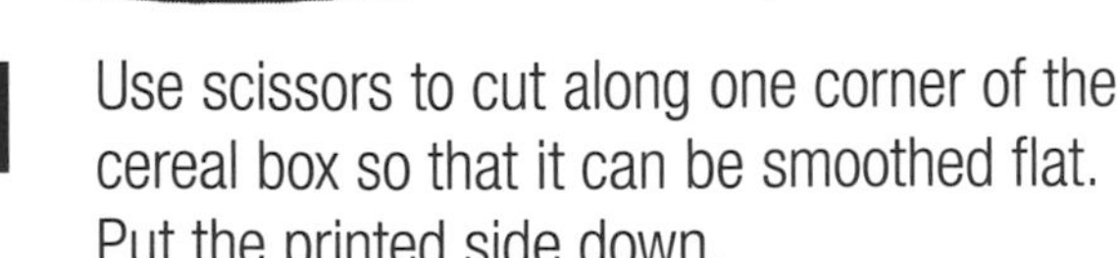

1 Use scissors to cut along one corner of the cereal box so that it can be smoothed flat. Put the printed side down.

2 Using a pencil and ruler, draw one side of the structure. The side should not be a rectangle—instead it should taper near the top. The width of the base should be about 3½ inches. The height should be 11 inches. At the 10-inch point, the width of the side should be 2 inches; the top inch of the side should be in the shape of a triangle, with a point at the very top.

3 When you have finished measuring and drawing one side, cut it out. Use the first side to trace three more identical sides. Cut them all out.

4 Paint your monument on the plain cardboard side. The pictures and writing side will be hidden when you assemble the monument.

5 After the paint has dried, lay the four sides flat, with the painted (or plain) side facing down.

6 Tape one side to the next, until all four are joined. The triangle tips should not be taped. Fold down the triangle tips to make a crease where the triangle sits on the top of the monument.

7 Stand your four sides to form the monument. Attach the last two sides with tape. Complete the monument by folding the triangle pieces at the top to form a point. Secure with tape. Your monument is complete!

abolish: get rid of.

aide-de-camp: a military officer who acts as an assistant to a superior officer, usually a general or admiral.

alliance: a group that works together for a common goal.

allies: people who join together to help each other.

ambition: desire for achievement or distinction such as power, honor, fame, or wealth.

ambush: a surprise attack.

apprentice: someone in training.

archive: an extensive record or collection of papers.

armory: a storage place for weapons and other war equipment.

artillery: mounted guns, such as cannons.

bickering: arguing.

blockade: closing off a place or port to prevent entry or exit.

border disputes: when two parties argue over where land boundaries or borders fall.

bounty: a gift or generous supply of something.

boycott: to stop buying or using.

cabinet: a government leader's group of advisors.

checks and balances: a system of three branches of governments in which no one branch becomes too powerful. Each branch can be restrained by the other two.

clan: large family.

colleagues: associates.

colonial: the period of time when America was a group of British colonies from 1607 to 1776.

commander in chief: the person in charge of a country's military.

commission: a directive or assignment of an officer in the military.

constitution: a document containing the basic laws and beliefs of a country.

Constitutional Convention: the meeting in Philadelphia at which the government of the United States was created.

Continental Army: the army formed by the American colonies at the beginning of the Revolutionary War. This was the war for independence from Great Britain.

cooperage: a place where barrels or casks are made.

court: to spend time with someone and decide to marry.

cue: a small ponytail at the back of the head.

cupola: a dome-like structure on a roof, sometimes housing a bell or lantern.

delegation: a group of representatives.

demotion: reduced to a lower grade or rank.

diameter: the line through the center of a circle, from one side to the other.

distillery: a place where grains such as wheat and corn are processed into alcohol.

diversify: to produce many different crops or goods.

drafting: drawing or sketching.

edifice: a large, impressive building or organization.

edifying: uplifting.

emissary: a representative sent on a mission.

enlistment: the period of time a person is committed to military service.

epaulets: decorations on the shoulders of military uniforms.

estates: all of someone's property.

etiquette: accepted code of public behavior.

eulogy: a speech or writing in honor of a dead person.

executive: the branch of government that carries out laws.

expedition: a journey made for war or exploration.

fatally: leading to death.

Federalist: a political party in the late 1700s that favored a strong central government.

fervor: great feeling.

foreign affairs: relations with other countries.

Founding Fathers: members of the Constitutional Convention.

French and Indian War: the war between France and England for control over the colonies in America. It lasted from 1756 to 1763.

frontier: the land or territory that is the farthest part of a country's settled areas.

garrison: a military post where troops are stationed.

gentry: group of people with great wealth.

gristmill: a mill for grinding grain.

guardian: a person who protects and takes care of a child whose parents have died.

guillotine: a device that uses a heavy blade positioned between two posts to cut off a person's head.

heirs: children to leave his wealth to.

Hessian: professional German soldier hired by England.

horsemanship: skill in handling and riding horses.

House of Burgesses: assembly of representatives in colonial Virginia.

implicated: shown to be involved in a matter or a crime.

inoculation: vaccination to protect against a disease.

integrated: including members of different races, religions, and backgrounds.

judicial: the branch of government that administers justice.

knoll: a small rounded hill.

lease: rent.

legacy: knowledge passed on—what someone is remembered for.

legislate: to make or enact laws.

liaison: link or connection.

life mask: plaster cast of the face.

logistics: the planning and organizing of details for a business or military operation.

meticulous: very precise and taking extreme care with small details.

midshipman: an officer in training in the navy.

militia: a group of citizen soldiers; not professionals.

moderate: not following extreme views, especially in politics.

monarchy: rule by a king.

morality: conforming to rules of conduct.

mutiny: revolt or rebellion against authority.

neutrality: policy of not getting involved in a war between other countries.

obscurity: being unknown.

octagonal: eight sided.

old maid: a woman past the usual age of marriage.

oppressive: exercising power in a cruel and unjust way.

orphan: a child whose parents are both dead.

penmanship: the quality or style of handwriting.

pension: a fixed amount of money paid on regular intervals to older workers.

portico: a structure with a roof and columns, like a porch.

practical skills: useful skills to use every day.

precedent: a decision that serves as a guide for the future.

privateer: an armed ship that is privately owned but hired by a government to fight enemy ships.

raider: someone who makes a surprise attack.

ratify: to approve formally.

regiment: a group of military ground forces consisting of battle groups, headquarters, and support units.

Reign of Terror: a period of time during the French Revolution, from 1793 to 1794, when many people were killed by the ruling group.

reinforcements: more troops.

remedy: a healing medicine or treatment.

Republican: a political party in the late 1700s that supported state rights.

rheumatism: pain or stiffness of the back, arms, and legs.

schooner: a type of sailing ship with two or more masts.

secretary of state: the person in charge of foreign affairs.

siege: surrounding and attacking a fortified place, like a fort, and cutting it off from help and supplies.

skirmish: a brief fight between two groups.

smallpox: a deadly disease that leaves the skin scarred.

Stamp Act: a tax on paper goods produced in the colonies.

sterling: British money.

stockade: a solid fence made with strong posts standing upright in the ground.

strategic union: marriage for practical reasons.

summon: to call or notify to appear at a certain place.

surrogate: taking the place of somebody.

surveyor: someone who measures land areas to set up boundaries.

tinker: a mender of pots, kettles, and pans.

Townshend Acts: taxes on goods sold to the colonies by Great Britain.

tract: defined area of land.

traitor: someone who is disloyal and abandons or betrays a group or cause.

tranquility: calmness and peacefulness.

triumph: victory.

tuberculosis: a deadly disease of the lungs.

veteran: a former soldier.

visionary: able to anticipate the future and see ways of doing things before many others do.

widow: a woman whose husband has died.

★ RESOURCES ★

Books

Barton, David. *Bulletproof George Washington.* Wallbuilder Press, Aledo, TX, 1990.

Brookhiser, Richard. *Rediscovering George Washington: Founding Father.* Simon & Schuster, NY, 1997.

Bryant, Helen. *First Lady of Liberty: Martha Washington.* John Wiley & Sons, NY, 2002.

Ellis, Joseph. His Excellency, *George Washington.* Random House, NY, 2004.

Flexner, James Thomas. *Washington: The Indispensable Man.* Little, Brown, NY, 1969.

Grizzard, Jr., Frank. *143 Questions and Answers about George Washington.* Mariner Publishing, Buena Vista, VA, 2009.

Johnson, Paul. *The Founding Father: George Washington.* Harper-Collins, NY, 2005.

Washington, George. *George Washington Writings.* Library of America, 1997.

Web Sites

www.archives.gov
National Archives. Online copies of the Declaration of Independence, Bill of Rights and Constitution.

http://gwpapers.virginia.edu
The Papers of George Washington at the University of Virginia.

www.mountvernon.org
George Washington's Mount Vernon Estate and Gardens.

www.nps.gov/fone/index.htm
Fort Necessity National Battlefield

www.nps.gov/gewa/index.htm
George Washington Birthplace

www.nps.gov/vafo/index.htm
Valley Forge National Historical Park

www.pbs.org/georgewashington
Rediscovering George Washington, PBS.org

www.whitehouse.gov/about/presidents/georgewashington
Biography of George and other presidents from official White House site.

★ INDEX